OBSESSIONAL NEUROSIS

Despite the important place it occupies in both Freudian and Lacanian nosology, obsessional neurosis has received far less attention than its erstwhile companion hysteria. This book aims to elaborate and deepen research into questions of obsession, going beyond the usual clichés which reduce obsession to the question "Am I alive or dead?". Emphasis is given to the structure of this neurosis, as distinguished from its symptomatology, and to clinical questions of work with obsessional subjects. The chapters provide discussions of some of the following themes: the creation of the category of obsessional neurosis and of obsessive-compulsive disorder (OCD), the fate of desire and the inability to act in obsession, debt and guilt, obsessional manoeuvres and their implications for the treatment.

The book will be of interest to readers with academic or clinical backgrounds who wish to deepen their understanding of obsessional neurosis from a theoretical or clinical point of view. Newcomers to the subject will find signposts here that guide them through the complex landscape of obsession and lead them to avenues they may wish to pursue further.

Astrid Gessert is a psychoanalyst and a member of CFAR and of the College of Psychoanalysts-UK. She has worked for many years in the NHS, in private practice and as supervisor. She is a regular contributor to the CFAR public lecture and training programme and lectures and facilitates seminars at other psychoanalytic organisations.

THE CENTRE FOR FREUDIAN ANALYSIS AND RESEARCH LIBRARY

Series Editors:
Anouchka Grose, Darian Leader, Alan Rowan

CFAR was founded in 1985 with the aim of developing Freudian and Lacanian psychoanalysis in the UK. Lacan's rereading and rethinking of Freud had been neglected in the Anglophone world, despite its important implications for the theory and practice of psychoanalysis. Today, this situation is changing, with a lively culture of training groups, seminars, conferences, and publications.

CFAR offers both introductory and advanced courses in psychoanalysis, as well as a clinical training programme in Lacanian psychoanalysis. It can provide access to Lacanian psychoanalysts working in the UK, and has links with Lacanian groups across the world. The CFAR Library aims to make classic Lacanian texts available in English for the first time, as well as publishing original research in the Lacanian field.

OTHER TITLES IN THE SERIES

www.cfar.org.uk

OBSESSIONAL NEUROSIS

Lacanian Perspectives

Edited by Astrid Gessert

Routledge
Taylor & Francis Group

LONDON AND NEW YORK

First published 2018
by Routledge
2 Park Square, Milton Park, Abingdon, Oxon OX14 4RN

and by Routledge
711 Third Avenue, New York, NY 10017

Routledge is an imprint of the Taylor & Francis Group, an informa business

British Library Cataloguing-in-Publication Data
A catalogue record for this book is available from the British Library

Library of Congress Cataloging-in-Publication Data
A catalog record for this book has been requested

ISBN: 978-1-78220-458-9 (pbk)

Typeset in Optima and Palatino
by Apex CoVantage, LLC

CONTENTS

ACKNOWLEDGEMENTS

The following chapters have been published previously and are published with permission:

Castel's article "Guilty cognitions, faulty brains" has previously appeared in: Castel, P.-H. (2012). *La fin des coupables*, chapter VI: Cognitions coupables, cerveaux fautifs, pp. 355–384. Paris: Ithaque. It has been translated into English and is published in the present book with the author's and publisher's (copyright holder) permission.

Melman's article "The Rat Man" is the translation of a conference paper given by Charles Melman (Association lacanienne internationale) on 13th March 2016. It has been translated into English and is published in the present book with the author's permission.

Safouan's two articles "The signification of mastery of the control of the orifices in anal eroticism" and "The signification of debt in obsessional neurosis" have previously been published in Safouan, M. (1974). *Études sur l'Oedipe*, pp. 59–64 and 65–73. Paris: Seuil. They have been translated into English and are published in the present book with the author's (copyright holder) permission.

Silvestre's article "The Lacanian structure of obsessional neurosis" was published posthumously by his wife Danièle Silvestre in 2002 in *Revue Nationale des Collèges cliniques du Champ lacanien*: 135–156. Danièle Silvestre gave permission for the paper to be translated into English and published in this book.

ABOUT THE EDITOR AND CONTRIBUTORS

Luca Bosetti is a psychotherapist working in private practice in Nottingham and London. He has worked in the field of addiction and is currently training as psychoanalyst at the Centre for Freudian Analysis and Research (CFAR). He has written a thesis on Lacan and the ethics of psychoanalysis.

Pierre-Henri Castel, a philosopher and historian of science, is senior investigator at the National Center for Scientific Research (CNRS) in Paris, and a psychoanalyst in private practice, member of the Association lacanienne internationale (ALI).

Vincent Dachy practises and teaches Lacanian psychoanalysis in London. He is a member of CFAR and of the World Association of Psychoanalysis-New Lacanian School (WAP-NLS). Aside from psychoanalysis, he chases contrasts between sound, image, and writing in various compositions, between prose and poetry.

Astrid Gessert is a psychoanalyst and a member of CFAR and of the College of Psychoanalysts-UK. She has worked for many years in the NHS, in private practice and as supervisor. She is a regular contributor to the CFAR public lecture and training programme and lectures and facilitates seminars at other psychoanalytic organisations.

Darian Leader is a psychoanalyst practicing in London. He is a member of CFAR and of The College of Psychoanalysts-UK. His books include: *Why Do Women Write More Letters than They Post?*; *Stealing the Mona Lisa*; *Freud's Footnotes*; *What is Madness?*; *Strictly Bipolar*, and *Hands*.

Charles Melman is a psychoanalyst and psychiatrist working in Paris, and a founder member of the Association lacanienne internationale. He taught at the École freudienne de Paris, founded by Lacan, and was responsible for the journal *Scilicet*. He has recently published *L'homme sans gravité* (Denoël, 2002) and the seminars which he has been giving for many years have been published since 2010 by Eres.

Moustapha Safouan has practised psychoanalysis in Paris since 1949, and was one of the first students of Lacan. His many books include *Études sur l'Oedipe*; *Jacques Lacan and the Question of Psychoanalytic Training*; *Speech or Death*; *Why are the Arabs not Free – The Politics of Writing*; *Lacaniana*, and *La psychanalyse. Science, thérapie – et cause*. He is also the translator of Freud, La Boétie and Shakespeare into Arabic.

Michel Silvestre, who died in 1985, was a psychoanalyst and member of the École de la cause freudienne. One of the most esteemed of Lacan's students, his work is known for its clarity, precision and insight. A collection of his articles has appeared as *Demain la psychanalyse.*

PREFACE

Historically, obsessional neurosis has often been treated like the poor relative of the more flamboyant hysteria in clinical literature and research. This has changed over the last few decades, when the *Diagnostic and Statistical Manual of Mental Disorders* (DSM) became one of the main tools for diagnosing and treating different forms of human suffering in health services. The category of hysteria has disappeared altogether, and in the place of obsessional neurosis we find "obsessive-compulsive disorder" (OCD). This change is reflected in the huge number of people currently considered to suffer from OCD and being treated for it.

Recognising the implications of this change for the conceptualisation of obsessional neurosis, its diagnosis and treatment led to our wish to bring obsessional neurosis back on stage, with the aim of furthering the theoretical conceptualisation of this clinical structure and stimulating the discussion of its importance in the understanding of human suffering and its treatment.

The essays that have been selected in this book approach this subject from a psychoanalytic perspective, informed by the work of Jacques Lacan. They are meant to invite the reader on a guided tour through the landscape of obsessional neurosis, to pick up relevant themes and to develop ideas about questions concerning obsession and its treatment for further discussion and research, rather than to inform in a textbook like manner. This is particularly the case with regard to the articles of the French authors, which are sections of their larger works, either chapters from comprehensive books or papers relating to seminars that have been running over a period of time. It is hoped that readers may use the texts collected in this book as stepping stones for further exploration of the themes presented. As with much of the literature in the field of psychoanalysis, working through these essays by speaking about them, for instance in study groups and seminars, may be a particularly fruitful way to engage with their subject.

I would like to express my very special thanks to the authors for their generous sharing of their thoughts, and for giving their time and their permission to translate and use their texts in this book. Darian Leader promoted the initial idea of compiling a book on obsessional neurosis from a Lacanian perspective and provided, as always, unflagging and most helpful support throughout the entire editing process; I am greatly indebted to him. A big "thank you" goes to Lindsay Watson for her creative and excellent translations of the complex French texts, which often required informed interpretations rather than simple word-by-word transmissions of French into English, and for her equanimous patience with my many nitty-gritty questions. As always, it was very reassuring to know Pat Blackett being by my side to help with any on-line search and other tricky issues. Oliver Rathbone and the staff at Karnac provided much appreciated encouragement and easy-going support for the book in its early stages and Russell George and Naomi Hill at Routledge gave generously all the help that was needed in its publication, "thank you" to all of you.

Astrid Gessert

A brief outline of Freud's and Lacan's conceptualisation of obsessional neurosis

ASTRID GESSERT

Psychoanalysis started with Freud's research into hysteria, based on his work with his early patients, as he himself pointed out (Freud, 1913m, p. 209). This view is neglecting the fact, however, that from the beginning he differentiated hysteria from obsessional neurosis.

Already in his article on "The neuro-psychoses of defence" (Freud, 1894a), he distinguished conversion hysteria, where an incompatible idea is transformed into a somatic symptom, from "*Zwangsvorstellungen*" (obsessional ideas), where the affect that has been connected with an unbearable idea becomes attached to another, more acceptable idea, thus establishing a "false connection". This feature marks obsessional thinking.

Right from the start of his clinical studies, when he first thought that symptoms result from affects that could not be sufficiently discharged, Freud had recognised that at the root of neurotic developments are unacceptable ideas, and that affects are not abreacted through physiological processes or through action but through language. He argued that human beings can use language as the instrument of abreaction, and that in some cases speaking itself is the appropriate act, for instance when articulating a painful secret. Understanding the importance of this unique capacity of human beings to use speech when it came to abreacting what seemed to be purely concrete or physical issues became fundamental to the development of psychoanalysis.

When Freud abandoned hypnosis as a treatment technique and focused more closely on the speech of his patients, he recognised what became and remained his basic model of neurosis: it begins with a conflict between incompatible ideas (that often articulate erotic or hostile wishes), and ends, via repression of some of these ideas, in symptoms that provide a substitute satisfaction for the now unconscious wish.

Closer examination of the mechanisms involved in this process led him to distinguish different types of neurosis according to where and how this problematic finds its predominant expression: in the body (hysteria), as anxiety and avoidance strategies (phobia), or in thinking (obsession). The hallmark of obsessional neurosis are strategies staged in the realm of thinking: an unacceptable idea is replaced by another idea.

***

All authors of the articles in this book emphasise this structural feature of obsessional neurosis, the effect of language – Freud's "ideas" – on the subject, rather than the particular symptomatology that may follow from it. With this orientation they follow the understanding Jacques Lacan has developed of obsessional neurosis, which forms the basis of the arguments developed in the articles to follow.

From a Lacanian point of view, the fundamental plight of all human beings, or more precisely of all speaking subjects, is that we are subjected to the effect of language, to something that does not come from us but is "Other" to us. With the acquisition of language, a mythic primary condition that might be called "nature" is lost, yet language is the only means through which we can construct an identity and through which we can relate to the world and others. Having to represent ourselves and our world through language that comes from an Other means that inevitably something will be missed, a gap will occur leaving the subject divided between the way he represents himself and something unknown that cannot find representation. Lacan conceptualised this missing part as object *a*. From this lack, desire will emerge, in an effort to find completion. The missing object will function as the cause of this desire.

This desire is problematic, as completion, either by total immersion in the field of the Other or by total refusal to engage with the Other, would mean obtaining complete satisfaction, the dangerous enjoyment that Lacan calls jouissance, which would mean at the same time the end of the subject. The subject can only exist as marked by a split.

How this split and the desire arising from it is negotiated produces the basic clinical structures: neurosis, psychosis and perversion, and within the realm of neurosis, the forms of hysteria and obsession.

The basic structure of obsessional neurosis as understood in the Lacanian field of psychoanalysis evolves around the obsessional's specific relation to his lack and to desire. The obsessional manages his lack and the desire arising from it by denying it. This implies also that he denies that his lack, and the object that causes desire, has anything to do with an Other. In his fantasy he holds on to the object and tries to obliterate the Other to keep himself in an isolated state of self-sufficiency (see Fink, 1997, chapter 8).

Problems occur when he is confronted with the desire of the Other who is also lacking. The Other too is marked by a lack that cannot be filled, not by any subject. Being confronted with this lack produces anxiety in the obsessional (see here Melman & Silvestre). Because desire and the object causing it cannot be articulated, it leaves the obsessional in suspense as to what object he might be for the Other and at the peril of being exactly the object that would satisfy the Other, complete the Other, provide the Other with jouissance, which would mean that he would disappear as subject.

One way the obsessional may try to manage this situation is by splitting the Other into an Other of desire and an Other of demand and engaging only with the Other of demand by refusing to oblige. Thus, through refusing a supposed demand and obliterating the desire of the Other he sustains his own precarious desire as an impossibility (see here Bosetti).

The obsessional's fantasy about the demand of the Other is that the Other demands jouissance, a jouissance about which the obsessional does not want to know anything in terms of it belonging to himself. The obsessional is obsessed with jouissance and transfers it to the Other (see here Silvestre). The jouissance that he imagines the sadistic Other demands is the uncontrollable, wild jouissance that knows no limits, that is not regulated by the law of the father and castration; this is what the obsessional is attracted to while at the same time being terrorised

by. To defend himself against it, he clings to phallic jouissance, the jouissance that is marked by castration, but he refuses to pay the price of
castration (see here Dachy). He tries to tame it by keeping everything
equal: "I give you this, so that you can return that to me", and by meeting the injunctions that come from this Other place that he locates outside himself with immediate refusals. But ultimately, he fails to maintain
the balance and remains caught up in situations that are impossible to
resolve, e.g., by accepting a debt he has not incurred while making it
impossible to repay it (see here Silvestre & Safouan).

This scenario and its essential parameters – desire, the object, jouissance and debt – are examined in the articles of this book from various
angles. The authors elaborate the typical impasses the obsessional finds
himself in, the symptoms that are likely to arise in his manoeuvres, and
the implications for the treatment and for the position the analyst has to
take, often using the historical Rat Man case as illustration.

***

The notion of obsessional neurosis as an "idiom of distress" that
articulates a subject's particular attempt at resolving fundamental
questions of existence has been lost in the contemporary category of
obsessive-compulsive disorder (OCD) which has replaced the concept
of obsessional neurosis in non-psychoanalytic clinical approaches.
These contemporary approaches focus on the symptomatology rather
than on the structure of the clinical category, a shift which has far reaching consequences for the status and prevalence of this clinical picture
in society, as well as for its diagnosis and treatment (see here Castel &
Leader).

The collection of articles in this book goes against this trend and
invites further explorations of precisely those facets of obsessional neurosis that have been lost sight of as it became replaced by the category
of OCD.

***

In the opening article "Guilty cognitions, faulty brains" Castel
engages with the problematic development that led to the introduction
of OCD. His article is a chapter from his book *La fin des coupables* (2012)
in which he examines how the political, social, and cultural changes that

led in Western societies to a decline of communal structures and values and an enforced emphasis on individualism and autonomy transfigured the "maladies of civilisation and their therapeutic solutions".

While in Freud's time people were riddled with guilt and intrapsychic conflicts, the new demands for self-agency and self-control instigate a new relation to one's self, if not a new concept of self altogether, a self not tormented by contradictory tendencies and aspirations, but a cognitive self, even a "cerebral" self that creates and manages itself. With this development come new collective expectations of "well-being". Castel argues that it is these expectations, and not scientific or therapeutic progress, that led to the decline of psychoanalysis and the emergence of new forms of cognitive and behavioural therapies.

In the chapter selected for this book Castel examines more specifically the process in which "obsessional neurosis" became replaced by "obsessive-compulsive disorder" (OCD) since the 1980s and with the construction of *DSM III*. He regards this seemingly "minor detail" as a major event in the history of psychiatry which has far reaching consequences for "being oneself" and for collective expectations of "well-being", as well as for diagnosis and the development of new forms of treatment.

He argues that unlike traditional obsessional neurosis, OCD is no longer regarded as an "idiom of distress", that symptoms are not considered to carry meaning, and that it is no longer of interest how people experience their symptoms and how they speak about them. This trend culminates in the attribution of obsessions and compulsions to disturbances in cerebral functioning, to "faulty brains", and treatments aim at eradicating symptoms, rather than use them as stepping stones in the exploration of a person's complex history.

With the decline of obsessional neurosis emerges another way of "being oneself": In the "age of autonomy" being oneself means being the creator of oneself, being a creative agent who is at the centre of his actions, who is autonomous, takes self-control and self-responsibility. In this process of self-creation, guilt is no longer a "central referent"; guilt and anxiety are considered to be contingent disturbances of one's autonomy. And the imperative is not to remain fixed to one's creation of oneself, but to be reactive and flexible, to keep on changing who one is, engaging in a constant revision of one's life.

Along with these changed expectations and demands in the relation to oneself came an enormous increase in the number of people diagnosed with OCD since the 1980s. Castel discusses two trends to account for this increase:

1. Objectification: For the "post-guilt" generation psychic suffering is not considered to be one's fault, it is not seen as part of one's unique history, but as something objective one is afflicted with like an organic illness. The trend to objectify subjective experiences also informs the new diagnostic instruments in the form of *DSM* and other inventories that have been developed since the 1980s. These enable practitioners and patients to diagnose obsessive-compulsive disorders purely on the basis of listed symptoms, without taking into consideration the person's experience of and relation to these symptoms, their "internal struggle", and the subjective historical context in which the symptoms emerged. The illness as well as the patients have become standardised.

    Many people will experience typical symptoms without thinking of themselves as obsessional/compulsive. However, without the additional information of how these symptoms are experienced, without the criterion of intrapsychic conflict, anybody experiencing typical symptoms can now be classified as OCD even when they are not troubled by their symptoms.

    This leads to the second trend:

2. Normalisation: There is now a tendency to regard obsessions and compulsions as normal. What makes people suffer is not the obsessions/compulsions as such, but how they deal with them. If they are troubled by them, then people have to learn not what they might mean but how to "deal differently with" them. This is the realm of cognitive-behavioural therapies. And this is where the self returns, but now not as a self torn by intrapsychic conflict, but as an agent that regulates its own difficulties, its own guilt and anxiety.

In his article "Lacanian approaches to obsession", Leader takes up the theme of the problematic effect that the replacement of obsessional neurosis by OCD had on diagnosis and nosology. He shows that a diagnosis based on symptoms will lead to confusion of clinical categories, since many symptoms deemed to indicate obsessionality can be found in different clinical structures, especially in psychosis. Furthermore, such an approach loses sight of the different functions the same symptoms can have in different clinical categories, of structural features central to obsession, and of the way obsession is bound up with language.

Leader elaborates how, after Freud, essential features of obsessional neurosis have been re-conceptualised by Lacan and found articulation in certain "formulae" that have become popular mottos in Lacanian literature and practice: "Am I alive or dead?"; "The obsessional denies the desire of the Other"; "The signifier cannot absorb all of jouissance"; "The obsessional is waiting for the death of the master." Re-visiting these formulae, Leader argues that while they address the impasses that are constitutive of the obsessional structure they often have the unintended effect of being taken as ready answers, thus hindering further exploration of the question of obsession and of the complexity of this structure.

He argues that while these formulae converge on the salient feature of mortification – one of the central facets of obsession for Freud and Lacan – Lacan had approached this question from different angles that lead to a complex picture of the function of desire and guilt in obsessional neurosis that is not adequately captured by the popular formulae taken in isolation. First, Lacan had elaborated the obsessional's mortifying impasse in terms of his dilemma both to destroy and sustain the desire of the Other (in *Seminar V: Formations of the Unconscious*, Lacan,1957–1958; see also here Bosetti); then, by using Lévi-Strauss' formula for myth to articulate the subject's attempt to situate himself in a kinship structure riddled with "fault lines". This is where the function of guilt comes in: it aims, unsuccessfully, to provide the prohibition that has failed to establish boundaries in the symbolic structure.

Recognising the complexity of obsessional neurosis has implications for the treatment. It is not only a question of elaborating the relation of the obsessional to the traumatic encounter with too much jouissance but of exploring the "fault lines" in the subject's history and exposing the structural, symbolic guilt which cannot be redeemed, but supports the subject in finding his place.

The function of fault and guilt in obsessional neurosis, and its relation to desire and not-knowing is the central question of Safouan's article "The signification of debt in obsessional neurosis". Freud had observed that unconscious wishes exist in the "not known" as a result of repression. Not knowing about a desire is the condition of its existence. Guilt arises when the truth of the repressed desire is approached; it blocks the way.

Safouan turns to the Rat Man to elaborate this: the father's fault, his unpaid debt, returns to haunt the son in the form of the captain who asks the Rat Man to pay back the sum for the postage of his glasses to Lieutenant A, who, however, had not laid out the money. The Rat Man knows the captain has made a mistake but represses this knowledge. He vows to fulfil the request to the letter, in blind obedience, while at the same time staging his revolt by producing an absurd condition that makes it impossible to fulfil the request.

By repressing knowledge, he keeps his desire intact. He burdens himself with an imaginary debt that cannot be paid back, sustaining an impossibility and refusing to recognise the symbolic debt that, for every subject, is transmitted from the father. Thus, he also sustains his jouissance.

The problematic relation of the obsessional with desire is also the focus in the article by Bosetti and in the second article by Safouan. In his essay "The cutting edge of desire in obsessional neurosis: Lacan with Leclaire", Bosetti elaborates how the obsessional's relation to desire creates a particular impasse, how he tries to resolve this, and what the implications of this scenario are for clinical practice.

Taking Lacan's proposition that central to the structure of obsessional neurosis is the subject's relation to desire (*Seminar V: Formations of the Unconscious*, 1957–1958) as starting point, Bosetti focuses on the particularity of this desire and the difficulties it produces for the obsessional subject. The obsessional strives to sustain a "pure" desire that is independent of the Other, that asks and expects nothing of the Other, that annuls the Other as point of address. but since the Other is the very place and source of any desire, the obsessional, by following his "pure desire" that annihilates the Other, risks at the same time the extinction of his desire. Hence, he has difficulties to sustain desire.

The obsessional's symptomatic solution is, as in any neurosis, a compromise. He attempts to split the Other into an "Other of demand" and an "Other of desire". By setting up the Other of demand who introduces rules and prohibitions, and who is endowed with rationality and consistency, the obsessional destroys the unpredictable and unfathomable Other of desire. While submitting to the set of rules and prohibitions of the Other of demand he can keep his desire alive as an impossible desire.

Bosetti illustrates how this particular relation to desire is played out in obsessional neurosis by turning to Leclaire's case of Philo, a patient who, by plugging up the desire of the mOther, could sustain his desire only in the form of inhibitions. Following Lacan's seminar on the *Formations of the Unconscious*, Leclaire had used this case material to illustrate the application of Lacan's structural approach in the clinic of obsessional neurosis.

This case study also highlights how desire must enter psychoanalytic practice by way of the analyst, in order to unravel the obsessional's fixation to a fantasy that plugs up and annuls the desire of the Other and hence inhibits his own articulation of desire.

Desire is again the focus in Safouan's article "The signification of mastery of the control of the orifices in anal eroticism". Safouan examines the link between desire and the law. He argues that the ideal of mastery that obsessionals pursue in their attempts at control, symbolised in behaviours relating to excretory functions, does not express a will to power; rather it is a defence against the overwhelming jouissance that haunts the obsessional subject. The obsessional locates jouissance in the anal region of his own body through his fantasy that it is the Other who seeks jouissance there and who has a malicious will to take him by force. This will of the Other appears as a demand, presented as a commandment, as an unmotivated malicious law dictated by the Other. Being confronted with this law evokes in the subject the desire to refute it, to become the lawmaker himself. The transfiguration of the law that is imputed to the Other into the desire of the subject to make the law is what fuels the obsessional's attempts at mastery. He mistakes his refusal to submit to the law for self-mastery, in the face of a jouissance that is far from being mastered.

Melman's article relates to his wider exploration of the function of language in obsessional neurosis which he had developed in the context of his seminar on the Rat Man case over a period of two years (1988–1989; Melman, 2015). Taking the structure of language and Lacan's teaching on this subject as his main point of reference, he argues that obsessional thinking, which is where, according to Freud, the obsessional's defence against unconscious desires becomes manifest, illuminates the essential way in which thinking functions for every subject; hence, what we can learn from obsessional neurosis concerns everyone (Delafond, 2002).

In the conference paper presented in this book Melman conceptualises the problem of the obsessional in terms of his difficulty to keep the object that yields jouissance at bay while at the same time refusing to renounce this jouissance and to make do with a substitute that would inevitably fail to fill his lack.

Melman elaborates and illustrates this understanding by referring to the Rat Man case. As a child, the Rat Man had crawled under the skirts of his nannies and seen the real thing, not the semblance that makes it desirable. He has indulged in voyeuristic jouissance, and then he loses his glasses, his way of seeing, and does not know if he should look for them or not, and if and how to pay for them. It leaves him in doubt and it is impossible for him to decide what to do. He is caught up in a binary choice, without a third point of reference.

This impossibility manifests itself in the form of injunctions, and the subject's immediate refusal: "You must ..." – " Don't ...". The obsessional is persecuted by injunctions that come from the object that should be expelled, but that has not been ejected. The object has remained wedged between signifiers; not being itself a representation but the real Thing, it has remained connected to representations and hence cannot be truly repressed but only be kept at a distance. This is the only defence the subject has against its intrusion. The obsessional tries to keep it at a distance by the operation of isolation, cutting the link between signifiers, while at the same time filling every supposedly empty space that would confront him with lack, and hence with his subjectivity.

In the article "The Lacanian structure of obsessional neurosis" Silvestre expands on the obsessional's problems *vis-a-vis* the desire of the Other and jouissance with the particular aim of illuminating the passage from the triggering of the neurosis to the entry into analysis, and the implications for the place occupied by the analyst, the direction of the treatment and its pitfalls.

He argues that neurosis is triggered when there is an encounter with the real of jouissance, when the real hits psychic reality and unsettles the precarious "balance between imaginary and symbolic" that the subject has achieved. Using the Rat Man as an example, he shows how the encounter with the captain, who for the Rat Man incarnates the Other's superegoical demand for jouissance, evokes something the subject feels irresistibly attracted to, yet something he cannot bear; he responds with overwhelming anxiety. The breach of jouissance introduces a *"Zwang"* (compulsion) – "you must" – to return to this jouissance. It terrorises him, he wants to know nothing about it. He tries to manage this catastrophe that unhinges his world by producing symptoms, in the case of the Rat Man through the evocation of contradictory injunctions that are impossible to fulfil. The symptoms are bound to fail to restore equilibrium, because the gap that has opened up through the eruption of the real can never be filled.

The failure of the symptoms leads to the entry into analysis, where the subject finds a place where speech, and a "subject-supposed-to-know", can be addressed. The work in the analysis can take two possible directions:

1. The subject finds a new support in the form of the analyst, whom he regards as arbitrator, as one who provides the rules and regulates the threatening jouissance. Thus, he strives to establish a new equilibrium at the price of his neurosis, of renouncing his subjectivity.
2. The analyst refuses to provide support and emphasises instability, division, and subjectivity, with the possibility of separating the subject from object *a*, and of bringing the subject closer to his truth, to his knowledge about jouissance.

Finally, Dachy takes the reader onto a carousel – not for the faint-hearted! – from symptom to fantasy to drive to fantasy and to symptom again ... and on this journey gives us a taste of the disjunction between "too much" and "not enough" that is so characteristic of the obsessional's plight.

He takes up the argument that the obsessional is subjugated to an excess of enjoyment which, inevitably, is forever failing to provide "global satisfaction". He elaborates how the obsessional tries to overcome this disjunction by restoring continuity in his fantasy and how, when the fantasy fails, symptoms are produced to minimise this failure.

These manoeuvres are reflected in the obsessional's defensive strategies and in the way he engages with desire. As desire functions as indicator of the impossibility of satisfaction and of restoring continuity, which is precisely what the obsessional wants to deny, he keeps desire itself in a state of impossibility, while assenting to an enjoyment of which he imagines himself to be the master. His typical delaying tactics testify to the attempt to postpone the realisation of desire and an encounter between desire and enjoyment, which would bring him face to face with the disjunction between the two.

The problem with finding satisfaction is also staged in the acrobatics of the obsessional's thinking and he finds support for it in the surplus so central to capitalist discourse, that is not only affine to the discourse of the obsessional, but pervades many facets of present day society.

Here, Dachy touches on the question of "how we all became 'normal' obsessionals" – raised by Castel in his article at the beginning of this book – from a different angle.

Thus, the journey of exploring the complexities of obsessional neurosis goes on.

References

Castel, P.-H. (2012). *La fin des coupables. Vol. II*. Paris: Ithaque.

Delafond, N. (2002). Comment lire l'Homme aux rats. *Revue L'Évolution psychiatrique, 67*: 199–206.

Fink, B. (1997). *A Clinical Introduction to Lacanian Psychoanalysis*. Cambridge, MA and London: Harvard.

Freud, S. (1894a). The neuro-psychoses of defence. *S.E., 3*. London: Hogarth, 1962, 41–68.

Freud, S. (1913m). On Psycho-Analysis. *S.E., 12*. London: Hogarth, 1958, 205–212.

Lacan, J. (1957–1958). *The Seminar of Jacques Lacan, Book V, Formations of the Unconscious*. J.-A. Miller (Ed.), R. Grigg (Trans.). Cambridge: Polity, 2017.

Melman, C. (2015). *La névrose obsessionelle*. Toulouse: Érès.

CHAPTER ONE

Guilty cognitions, faulty brains

Obsessive-compulsive disorders in the age of the condition-of-autonomy (1980–2010)

PIERRE-HENRI CASTEL

> Obsessions express a generalised disorder of activity, that is all they do: one day we will reach the point of appreciating the value of obsessional individuals and their psychological states because of the wide range of insight they offer us. (Pierre Janet, 1926, p. 43)

This chapter appears under the sign of a paradox. It will not tackle the consequences of the emergence and the domination of a new form of affective sensitivity; on the contrary, it will address the decline, or in any case, the relegation to a subordinate position of something whose pre-eminence since the seventeenth century had been highlighted elsewhere.[1] "The end of the guilty ones" obviously does not signify the end of guilt itself, either as a moral feeling or as a normative principle, but denotes its declassification within the scale of values. From this follows a change in the relation to the self, from the point of view of the spiritual, moral, psychological, and medical care that for a long period of time was associated with excesses of guilt. If guilt has lost its primacy in our moral economy, it is because a new form of individuation has been imposed on us. It is quite possible that this is barely perceptible to those whom it affects. As always in a "society of individuals", each one tends

1

to believe that the processes of individuation, including all the accidents and impasses that contribute to them, only concern individuals taken one-by-one. No-one seems spontaneously to conceive that being an individual is a social form, and this failure in comprehension occurs not because people are stupid or blind, but because it is precisely what it means to belong to "the society of individuals": to attribute to oneself, *as a value*, the status of creative agent within society ... which, *in fact*, socialises you as an individual-who-thinks-he-produces-himself. This new form is what we call the condition-of-autonomy. The aspiration-to-autonomy gave primacy to guilt, but that is no longer the case with the condition-of-autonomy.

These autonomies and distinct versions of individualism do not follow on from one another like Kuhn's paradigms, where in practice the new replaces the old or renders it unintelligible. The condition-of-autonomy does not eliminate the aspiration-to-autonomy: quite the contrary! They overlap one another, and the new one extends beyond the old one only at the very edges; to a significant degree they are co-extensive. What is more, the new one often contributes to the preservation of the old one, and even reinforces it in certain respects, by assigning new social and moral functions to it. This means that clear chronological cut-off points are made impossible. The same is of course true of the confusions concerning the great anthropological formations. Perhaps you recall the case Lacan made in the 1950s for a "scrupulous woman", Mary of the trinity, as if she had re-emerged from a forgotten seventeenth century. Having looked at the available documentation, you might even have the feeling that Lacan was trying out his idea of the subjection to the Other on her, as well as that of the necessity of separation, given that he gave such primacy to the drama of the "vow of obedience" in formulating his version of obsessions, rather than to sexual repression, which was where a more banal form of psychoanalysis had gone astray (Lacan,1950/2008, p. 14).This is an extreme case: the possibility of a "scrupulous" life in the midst of democratic modernity makes the living horizon of obsessionality recede to its very origins – and proves that those origins have not been forgotten "in spirit", at least where a few exceptional souls are concerned. With very good reason, at the moment when I am about to speak of the decline of obsessional neurosis and the emergence of obsessive-compulsive disorder (OCD), I want to emphasise strongly that there are still patients who are very similar to the Rat Man, not just in terms of their symptoms but in the very texture of their psychical being; in other words, there are still obsessionals for whom the Freudian Oedipus retains its full value. But for the purposes of analysis, I am obliged to favour, and unfortunately even to idealise, the limit-situations [*situations-limites*]: situations in which one can behave *as if* the condition-of-autonomy replaced the aspiration-to-autonomy. All of a sudden, the malaise of being civilised, in other words, of being constrained to be oneself [*Selbstzwang*],[2] which from the very start I have set up in opposition to the aging themes of the history of western "subjectivity" or of "self-care", gives us a sense that *another sort of human being is making its appearance*. This is an exaggerated impression, and it is an artefact inherent in the methodology. Placing the accent on psychopathology serves only to augment it, and it produces a kind of anti-hero of contemporary psychical transformations, which both fascinate us and at the same time hide the extent to which the ancient practices associated with guilt still endure. So, we have continually to work against the false impression that has given rise to my quest for an ideal type of the post-guilty human being.

On the other hand, I fully accept that ancient forms of the inability to act continue to exist among the new ones. But this persistence does not prevent it from being true that the limits to change the relation to one's self are reflected in the new *psychotherapies* for guilt and anxiety, or indeed in the causes that are attributed to those states (whether by popular psychology or by neuroscience). I am going to presume that those therapies respond to a functional need. In examining them, we may discern the change of meaning, and even of the psychological scope, of both anxiety and guilt. These affects will no longer be anything more than *contingent* disturbances of our autonomy (I am running ahead of myself here, as this is what I shall conclude later). In this respect, the eradication of psychoanalysis and the dominance of cognitive-behavioural therapies (CBT) for obsessive-compulsive disorders will become strategic wagers – which will have no less epistemological dignity than the radical changes in work or family life. Where the condition-of-autonomy is concerned, let us say that the symptoms of obsessionals no longer constitute a language of distress that can be understood by everyone. They no longer haunt the psychical life of just anyone. They no longer open a window on to the mysteries of the soul. But while they are no longer the province of great literary models, neither are they psychical defects that endanger public freedoms, that afflict entire classes of persons who are too rational, too rigid. For a whole group of people, they are no different from a migraine or a stammer: a "hiccup in my brain". It feels more and more forced, even anti-scientific, to attribute meaning to them. And when clinicians come up against the banal fact that patients overvalue their obsessions, they conclude that, in the final analysis, this is due to cognitive bias. It is a pseudo-reason born of ignorance of the true causes. Worse than that: far from making it intelligible, this ethical over-valuation is part of the symptom. Eradication is the touchstone of treatment: you just have to stop believing that you are "abnormally" guilty, responsible, etc. From the point of view of Loudun's possessed, Kierkegaard in Copenhagen, or Freud in Vienna[3], what a reversal! However, let us not fall into the trap of bewailing the decline of the clinic, or even a veiled dehumanisation of the neurotic experience. *From the debris of the old language of obsessional distress, a new one is gradually re-forming.* One day I may flesh out this idea – not so much in order to establish facts of an anthropological nature, in some kind of "science of OCD", but rather to outline the ordinary moral practice of the new obsessionals.

I will begin by sketching out a number of social, political, and cultural facts that have been enmeshed in the fabrication of autonomy since the 1980s. This will enable me to establish a context for approaching the new therapies for unwellness.

In the mid-1970s, the last vestiges of authoritarianism disappeared from Europe (the death of Salazar, then of Franco, the fall of the Greek Colonels). During the night of the 9th-10th November 1989 (the anniversary of Hitler's Munich putsch) the Berlin Wall fell – this was *die Wende*, the turning point. A peace treaty was signed with the Soviet Union in September 1990 – this had not happened before. Within a few months, the communist bloc was falling apart. On 26th December 1991, the Soviet Union was dissolved. The end of the Cold War was such a triumph for liberal democracies and for capitalism that many felt it was simply "the end of history". The ascent of China (by 2010 the second most powerful economy in the world) and the emergence of a multipolar world took some time to establish themselves as givens. And as well as terrorism, other forms of insecurity (ecological accidents, the threats of climate change[4]) were added to the collective anxiety typical of the Cold War era: the idea of a nuclear holocaust.

The socio-political changes have been profound. Around 1980, the Keynesian welfare states, which had guaranteed growth and the redistribution of wealth since 1945, began to reach the end of the line. The gains in productivity, which were lower than they had been during the thirty golden years following World War II, were no longer correlated either to a rise in salaries in real terms, or to an increase in the number of jobs. Ronald Reagan and Margaret Thatcher stopped subsidising industry, curtailed the power of the trades unions, opened all markets up to competition, and introduced cuts to state bureaucracies. The post-state management style of *new public management* took the place of the ideal of justice of the welfare state. This led to the conjunction of widespread deregulation, the delegation of public power to private entities, and the investment of individuals with responsibility. They were allowed to get on with it in an autonomous fashion, and more and more frequently, if there was still State control, it was subsequent to the execution of the delegated tasks. Moreover, *new public management* aimed for good, flexible management of the fits and starts of the economic situation rather than for orderly distribution of the fruits of weaker economic growth. For those who found themselves excluded by these neoliberal policies, the welfare state shrunk to fit the format of a *workfare state* which enjoyed ever-diminishing support, just as much in the middle classes as in the social-democratic parties, which had spearheaded the democratic individualism of the 1960s. Indeed, a ransom was now paid for the Keynesianism of the preceding phase in the form of an explosion of budgetary deficits. The ruination of the socialist counter-model in the Eastern Bloc left the progressive parties with no alternative when they were faced with the return of the flame of political and economic liberalism, which had been virtually extinguished in the 1960s. Autonomisation, understood over a long period as political emancipation that was carried out *collectively*, suddenly became discredited.

It was in this context that autonomy, understood *a contrario* as an egotistical turning in on oneself, appeared to triumph. The condition began to spread. I refer, for example, to Lasch's 1979 book, *The Culture of Narcissism: American Life in an Age of Diminishing Expectations*, which gave a bleak account of the sixties. It was read more and more widely as being prophetic: individuals were going to become more and more "narcissistic". The 1990s were to see new kinds of psychical plagues emerging, against the backdrop of the media, which only served, apparently, to confirm his view. Late-nineteenth-century psychiatrists wondered whether kleptomania was compulsive or impulsive. Another version of this phenomenon, impulse buying ("shopaholism"), presented the dilemma anew: between two per cent and ten per cent of the population were supposed to be victims of this syndrome, and of those, between eighty per cent and ninety-five per cent were women, all of whom were anxious and depressed. To an ever-greater extent, body image was becoming a key factor in the construction of autonomy. Epidemics of anorexia nervosa and anorexia-bulimia followed from the 1980s onwards, exploding with particular ferocity in former "developing" countries where prosperity was replacing privation. A striking feature of this pathology is the sublime value that patients give to the absolute control they have over themselves. This can go as far as a complete denial of the illness as such, supported by the vocabulary of the unassailable autonomy of the relation to one's self and to one's body. To such an extent did the vocabulary of the ego achieve the status of normative evidence in the self-description of psychical life, that we could describe the 1980s epidemic of "multiple personality disorders" in the United States as a *social* symptom of the impossibility of dealing with the tug-of-war between the various poles of desire, other than by giving each one a "personality". So, each one would have a sort of legitimacy to express itself autonomously. Was the ego collapsing under its own weight? The majority of these mass pathologies (depression being their culmination) affect more women than men. It is tempting to explain this by making the contemporary feminine condition the laboratory for the constraints of the condition-of-autonomy. I am speaking, of course, of women who are politically and economically in a position to benefit from it and therefore also to suffer from it. To this we can add a striking fact – that OCD is equally distributed between men and women, whereas part of the understanding of *Zwangsneurose* was that it was men (sons) who were the designated victims. With the progressive equalisation of the conditions of the genders, there is no longer the slightest reason to make out that there is something especially masculine about this kind of activity.

At the same time, everything was happening as if the individual were re-appropriating for himself the principles of the bureaucratic regulation of the 1960s (non-directive planning) and as if he were becoming a self-regulating entity assuming the calculation of his own risks. The liberal ambition to bring about the decline of the state was now beginning to resonate with the ambition to encourage the *self-government* of the individual by the individual – basically, *self-government*, once it is taken into the private domain, becomes *self-management* of each individual by himself. From then on, the rules of collectivism were considered to be counter-productive and clumsy, even to the extent of becoming shackles. In short, the gains of the post-war years, which enabled the mass emergence of the democratic individual through universalising access to healthcare, education, paid work and consumption, lost its legitimacy. Many privileged individuals, who owe their triumphant individuality and their autonomy to this historical process, are turning against it and disavowing it. Some of them even resent the rich institutional environment which gave them access to an unprecedented individualisation of their existence, as a burden from which they aspire to free themselves. Why should you prescribe something to an individual that he can perfectly well do for himself, and decide on for himself? In their eyes, self-constraint is so deeply rooted in the experience of autonomy, that any constraint imposed from "outside" (and the "outside" for such individuals is, of course, the social!) would be something that one had ultimately to be emancipated from, and would therefore be considered alienating. So, the old "obsessional" discipline, which was a point of honour for anyone integrated into the 1960s, could become transformed into a danger: the danger of lacking "reactivity" in a competitive universe. Richard Sennett, akin to Erikson and Riesman, saw in this a psychological threat to the contemporary individual (Sennett, 2006).

So, values, but also the great mechanisms at play in the way society is organised, reflect these economic and political twists and turns. As the hierarchical and integrative forms of the organisation of industrial society have undergone a slow decline, the worker's status has changed. In a society in which production is the work of individuals called upon to carry out tasks which become more and more autonomous, and even to self-manage from one project to the next, the subjectivisation of economic roles has become the norm. Even the Toyota model, which has taken over from the Ford model of industrial production, rests on the responsibility accrued by the agents [kaizen]; both the engineer and the person on the assembly line now take part in diagnosing and solving problems. This accrual of responsibility has a bizarre echo in the new way that machines function, for example, stopping themselves working when the quality of the product falls too low. This is called "autonomation" [jidoka]. More generally, believing in this, being "reactive" and flexible, encourages everyone, and all the more those who are young and qualified, to blur the boundary between personal and professional investment. This puts one particularly strong trend into perspective: the shortening of the average working day. The worker is an individual who is permanently "pre-occupied" – indeed, worried. The once-powerful professionalised and politicised unions are in decline; protests and demands are often nowadays the concern of less formal movements. The individualisation of remuneration is having an effect at ever-lower levels in the hierarchy. These days, jobs have an ever-reduced sense of craft or status. Training often emphasises the need to learn and continue learning anew. The notion of the wage-earner, once the norm for social and professional integration in industrial society, where the ideal form was employment in public service, is now accused of being an obstacle to the flexibility of the production process. The division of labour, therefore, does not so much lead mechanically to the emergence of vast abstract classes of agents who recognise themselves as part of a collective destiny (workers, executives, employees, etc.), who would share a habitus and even show each other a degree of solidarity. On the contrary, co-operative encounters, all the while becoming more and more densely attended, are also more episodic. They obey the logic of networks, which are built and dismantled, rather than that of organigrams with fixed hierarchies. The privatisation of entire swathes of the public sector, and symmetrically, the rapid de-bureaucratisation of the vast companies extant in the 1960s, have thus forced many people to confront challenges at great personal cost. And yet, while many are suffering, more and more of the individuals involved are finding the new ways liberating, and view the framework of the old industrial system, of the German-style organisation, or its American-style managerial extensions, as alienating. Maybe it is utopian, the notion of the self-employed entrepreneur working only from home, sitting in front of a laptop, contactable "24/7" on his mobile, managing his private capital of skills within a fluid contractual framework, with very little interference in the way he organises his work, incarnating the imaginary "worker of the future" – we should be horrified, we should get him to give up his vows! From the employers' point of view, autonomy at work is thus considered to be a resource of productivity, while employees consider it as a subjective reward, or even as a mode of recognition, to the extent that new constraints and new types of malaise develop from it. In this context, the best educated people feel they have the right to supervise their supervisors and share their own expertise with experts; understanding what one "consents" to is emerging as a natural right. But knowledge justifies itself in a debate from which the argument from authority is excluded. Because traditional authority no longer reassures; rather it is a sign of weakness and irrationality. The consequences in the world of work are immense, for sure; but also in education, in the couple, in the relation to medical doctors, in the relation to justice and to politics.

These new behaviours are rooted in a new demographic deal in which the family, work and health have determining effects on one another in quite original ways. Since the 1980s, the ageing of the population has brought about a well-documented challenge in terms of social care in developed societies. But the impact of the new rhythm of existence on the way life unfolds is no less crucial. The reduction in the age of puberty has sexualised childhood in such a way that the reasons for sexuality becoming "unconscious", as was the case at the beginning of the twentieth century, hardly pertain any more. Adolescence has been remodelled by the lengthening of the period of education. As people are remaining younger much longer, they can know several different lives, have several families, move house often, move abroad from time to time. Re-making one's life may turn out to be an adventure or a disaster – it is never banal, to be sure, but it is always an *ordinary* event. This autonomy, which allows, but also insists on, the constant revision of career projects, also has a counterpart in one's love life. The more autonomous one is (and it is not simply a function of social class), the more this interweaving of private and professional trajectories becomes a source of opportunities; the less autonomous one is, the more one suffers. This is why more and more individuals aspire to autonomy, while at the same time they suffer on a daily basis from its peculiar negative impacts – forms of alienation that leave them perplexed. The result is that identities become more and more fragile; but the fragility is equivocal. Because to be able to "change who you are" is also a power, even a talent that can be commoditised. It seems that this power, or rather this obligation, to change who you are, but at the same time to be the "author of your own change" inflects the moral and psychical economy of individuals in the age of the condition-of-autonomy in a significant way. It was one thing to aspire to become oneself; quite another to have to keep re-inventing oneself incessantly in a "liquid" environment, to use Zygmunt Baumann's expression.

Therefore, we notice that there are three inflections to this, which I emphasise because they have well-known effects on the inability to act and on demands for psychical care. The first is that it becomes problematic to countenance the idea of destiny or the impression that life has meaning, along a tranquil path leading from childhood through adolescence to adulthood and then to old age. It is no longer possible to see which ideal identification (even with the Freudian father) could be of value throughout a trajectory which henceforth is devoted to twists and turns, to the unforeseen alterations of the forced reconstruction of the self. Knowing how to dis-identify, if I dare say so, is both a resource and a test. The second is the ever-increasing weight of affects linked to authenticity, as an antidote to the fragility of identities. More and more often, they are what constitute "the" moral life for us. To be fully one-self, following the condition-of-autonomy regime, no longer leads to mere self-fulfilment. It is the way to bloom, to blossom. The movement which began in the 1960s, with the "leisure society", has infiltrated all the springs of our actions. One result of this is that rather than pursuing an ideal, people assume that they have unexploited potential. For example, they no longer seek to become an artist, which involves the romantic risk of being an exception, but rather to "develop their creativity", and everyone has the right to do so. And the third inflection? This is the wavering in which individuals of the age of the condition-of-autonomy (at least, those who have the means to live in this way) seem to be caught up, between demanding normality and demanding singularity. The recurring paradox whereby each individual believes he is an individual of his own creation, whereas there is no greater social imperative than the insistence on becoming more and more individualised, reaches the point of paroxysm. The individual is torn between the anguishing sense of being abnormal in situations that are too singular, and the rejection of the impersonal conformity of situations that are too normalised. Here is one of a hundred examples: medical doctors are required to use protocols that are evidence based and therefore universally applicable; but at the same time patients demand treatment that is tailored to the most specific singularities of their condition. Conversely, people are prepared to trust themselves to those who promise the absolute personalisation of treatment for their physical or moral maladies; but only on condition that they are legally protected from any possible form of abuse, and that absolutely nothing abnormal should ever happen. There are plenty of similar examples in the spheres of education, work and the law – and even of sexuality.

These three difficulties pertaining to identity (no life can be lived to the end with the support of just one ideal; the quest for complete self-development and the primacy of authenticity; and the dialectic of

normality/singularity) can be found again at the heart of the care people deem to be right and proper for the treatment of their most intimate
unwellness. In fact, they reflect the confusion into which they have been
thrown by the new regime of post-industrial cooperation; this is my
hypothesis in the pages that follow.

Because we are right in the midst of it, and therefore do not have a
perspective as such, this is much harder to document than what I have
explained up to now. I am not claiming to give an exhaustive portrait of
our time, but simply to sketch out certain modifications on the horizon
of contemporary autonomisation and, of course, this is only for those
whom it concerns (without playing down, for example, the very real
persistence of poverty, or of massive disparities between nations). Obviously, I am giving a picture centred on the middle classes who are able to
have recourse to psychotherapies. It is in this social and material milieu
that both the maladies of civilisation and their therapeutic solutions are
mutually engendered. In any case, it is the historical framework of our
time within which one may suffer from the incapability to act and to
cooperate with others "completely autonomously". So, I will now focus
down further, so that we can see the extent to which this incapability
is not just another affliction among others, but a perpetual crisis for the
democratic individual.

Let us not, however, lose sight of the paradox I started out with. On
the one hand, indeed, in this very broad context, obsessions and compulsions occupy a prime position in the palette of our woes. Through
their prevalence, which since 1980 has been estimated to be around
three per cent of any given life span, it is the fourth most widespread
mental illness, preceded (according to the research) by depression, phobias and anxiety states, and substance abuse. The cost of all this can be
calculated: by the end of the 1990s, anxiety disorders were costing more
than forty billion dollars annually in the United States of America.[5] On
the other hand, these figures say nothing of the form, whether exemplary or not, that a style of unwellness takes on in a world that is mor-
ally determined. Quite contrary to our expectations, it is only because
all sorts of individual behaviours and attitudes have been stripped of
their signifying attributes that the numbers have gone up. Deprived of
their specificity, they are easier to compile.

This is also why we see a clear point of departure: the gigantic quantitative leap in numbers of cases of OCD in the general population
before and after 1980. We know the reason for this. It was the American

research project called the "Five-city epidemiological study" carried out by Lee R. Robins, which was completed in 1984 after 20,000 people having been interviewed about all their mental symptoms, apart from dissociative disorders.[6] At that time, it was estimated that the prevalence of OCD over a lifetime was between 1.9 per cent and 3.3 per cent (the range has not varied) (Karno, Golding, Sorenson, & Burnam, 1988). What a surprise! As we recall, the figures for the 1960s were extremely low. Of course, everyone suspected that the figures had been underestimated. But no-one could have imagined that they would discover prevalence figures multiplied by twenty-five, or even sixty!

It would be pointless to attribute this explosion to a diabolical plot to create a market for the new psychotropic drugs. Lee Robins belonged to a generation of epidemiologists whose goal was to remove the stigma from mental illness by showing that it was far more widespread than had been supposed, and that generally it presented in forms that were far less serious than those of the popular imagination; but nonetheless they were medical conditions. For Lee Robins, the research project "Five-city study", which showed that one American in three suffered from some form of mental illness during their lifetime (particularly from depression and anxiety disorders), was not seeking any response in particular, and certainly not medication. The same was true for DSM-III: the fact of its being taken up by the pharmaceutical industry, a subject on which whole oceans of ink have been expended, only happened some years after its success.

So why was it that OCD, among all the disturbances that had been inventoried, was the one whose prevalence grew to this extent?

It was certainly not because the researchers had patiently explored the life histories of the interviewees, and uncovered from beneath the accumulation of reticence and embarrassed allusions the conflicts that were secretly ruining their lives. Quite the contrary: it was because the researchers had given the interviewees, key in hand, in the way their questions were formulated, the descriptions of the symptoms they were expecting. How could it have been otherwise? The researchers could not rely on the patients' spontaneous complaints. No, they had to help them to identify the disorders defined by the (future) DSM-III, even if they considered themselves to be neither unwell nor suffering. During the 1970s, the only list of obsessions and compulsions available in order to formalise such an enquiry was that of John E. Cooper (the Leyton Inventory; Cooper, 1970). So, it was made use of. But at no point was it thought necessary to include in the equation any discretion accorded to the obsessive-compulsives with regard to their symptoms (which included, as I recall, pathognomonic doubt: are my symptoms really symptoms?). An enormous number of people can present with behaviours that can be assimilated into OCD. But if they spoke freely about them, without shame or remorse, and if they did not integrate them into a global style of action and of a particular personality, a clinician of the 1960s would not have attributed them to an obsessional neurosis. Moreover, the study expanded to include age groups rarely examined before from the epidemiological point of view, in particular young people, who gave a high level of positive responses. The researchers who returned to these relatively unexplored age groups some years later, using the same methods, were astonished in their turn that anyone could have ignored for so long what to them seemed a public health problem that had been severely underestimated! In the 1980s, the mean age for the diagnosis of OCD was twenty years. By 2012, it was commonplace for OCD to be diagnosed at five or seven years of age. So, it was on the basis of typical symptoms, of subclinical intensity, inventoried from a wider population, and detached both from their social context and from the way they were experienced subjectively, that a figure for the prevalence of OCD twenty-five to sixty times greater than the previous one was reached. In itself, this would not pose a problem. If the aim was not to pathologise the ordinary, but to make something that had seemed to be severely morbid appear commonplace, then a quantitative leap of this sort can be deemed a success. It was believed that reducing the stigma meant easier access to treatment. But then it is equally logical to envisage the obverse – that there is also a risk of transforming disagreeable but transient episodes into mental illness: logical, yes, but additional factors are required in order for that formal possibility to become a medical or social reality.

Well, those additional factors were not long in appearing. I am now going to set-to and examine them. Here are the highlights of this final journey:

1. First of all, there was the weight of the new taxonomy of psychiatry. Because the definition of obsessions and compulsions in DSM posed some fearsome difficulties, which have by no means been resolved in the course of revisions of this great manual; quite the contrary.

2. It is impossible to understand these difficulties without taking into account the fact that cognitive-behavioural therapists and neuro-scientists have *de facto* challenged the definition of obsessions/compulsions in *DSM*, while at the same time constantly referring to it. Because the definition is categorical: it lists the symptoms which one needs to have in order to be affected by the disorder. Well, since the end of the 1970s, a completely opposing idea has emerged: there are such things as "normal" obsessions and compulsions which are experienced by everyone. Obsessive-compulsive disorder occurs if and only if individuals do not react to these so-called "normal" obsessions/compulsions as they should. This approach to symptoms can be defined as dimensional rather than categorical, since they can be more or less severe, and can range from normal to pathological. In my view, it is on this basis alone that justice can be done to the originality of cognitive-behavioural therapies for OCD; fundamentally, they aim to rectify the way the agent reacts, and even constructs him- or herself in relation to these "normal" obsessions/compulsions. I will give a broader socio-cultural context to this observation, because it goes a long way beyond the precise point at which these new therapeutic techniques for OCD are applied.

3. I will also explain how OCD was the testing ground for the frankly grandiose project of naturalisation, which mirrors the de-moralisation of obsessions. This will give us a chance to revisit tics and impulsive behaviours – themes that were already being discussed in the nineteenth century, but which were to take on a new importance. Because this naturalisation proposed norms other than moral ones for affects of a moral nature. Delving further into the details of CBT of OCD, we discover that they do not ultimately offer any explanations or the best therapies for our eternal difficulties, but rather seeks to shape people's minds so that their functioning and their norms of autonomy harmonise with the advances in neuroscience.

4. The way that OCD has been rendered cerebral, before our very eyes, is a real highpoint. How is it that obsessions and compulsions have ended up being reduced to functional disturbances of the basal ganglia? The answer cannot be exclusively epistemological. Because here it is not just a question of pure concepts; it is always

at the same time a question of collective representations, of images (even, indeed, of neuro-imaging!) and of expanding metaphors. So, we will also have to allow those people to speak who, from now on, find they are living with a "faulty brain", or to put it another way, with a reified interiority which does them harm, and may even wish them harm – which *wrongly* makes them feel guilty and anxious, because "they are doing everything right".

5. I will finish this overview with a plea in favour of the thesis that has underpinned everything I have discussed here: in the age of the condition-of-autonomy, guilt is no longer the central referent in the creation of individuality. The effacing of *Zwangsneurose*, which seemed like a minor detail in the history of psychiatry, and is so ill-understood from an anthropological point of view, to my mind signals the emergence of another way of being oneself, in other words, another form of being alive. In this regard, OCD is nothing but the debris of a language of distress that has passed away. As to what will re-form itself out of this debris – it remains an open question, as do the effects of the discourse that will take over from the old one, and that will doubtless be full of surprises.

Stock taking prior to liquidation: obsessions and compulsions in the age of *DSM*

In 1980, the third edition of the *Diagnostic and Statistical Manual* of the American Association of Psychiatry, *DSM-III*, was published; and this marked such a break with tradition in the history of the discipline that we forget the degree to which contemporary psychiatrists, including the man who oversaw the project, Robert L. Spitzer, were astonished by its success. As has been remarked, classification is a way of "fixing the boundaries of uneasiness" (Cottraux, 1998, p. 61). Since there is a vast amount of literature on the scientific style and the historical context of this book,[7] I shall concentrate here on the false simplicity of the way it defines obsessions/compulsions. Indeed, while the principles of identification of the disorder have scarcely changed since then (the fifth edition of *DSM*, due for publication in 2013, presages more serious developments, which I will return to later), very early on a conflict arose between those who held on to an "a-theoretical" description of OCD, and those specialist clinicians, therapists, and experimentalists who were convinced that they should keep their guns trained on the same target. While in the field of schizophrenia a sense of pessimism prevailed, very few experts in obsessions/compulsions were pessimistic. The definitions in *DSM-III*, which were still *stipulative* (they merely pointed out the meanings of words for the purposes of classification and, in that sense, were neither true nor false), were soon to be replaced by *real* definitions. The imminent discovery of the aetiology of the obsessions/compulsions would enable the correct treatment for them to be deduced.

So those are the main difficulties that appeared at that time.

I recall that the operationalised criteria of *DSM-III* had been tested in real life in the epidemiological Five-city study – suddenly propelling obsessions/compulsions to the forefront. This quantitative leap came into force in 1987, in the revised edition of *DSM-III* (R). In ninety-five per cent of cases, patients presented with both obsessions and compulsions; only around three percent had only obsessions, and rather fewer, two per cent, had only compulsions. In the 1990s, when the research was carried out for *DSM-IV*, following the great upsurge in the use of cognitive methods, it became apparent that there were far more pure obsessionals – perhaps twenty-five per cent. But the great majority remained in the obsessive-compulsive category. So, it was natural to start with the notion that patients presented with obsessions "and/or" compulsions. Paragraph 300.30 of *DSM-III*: "Obsessive-Compulsive Disorder (or Obsessive-Compulsive Neurosis)", which became paragraph 300.3 in *DSM-IIIR*, was worked out according to this principle. In a manual which was taken to be an anti-Freudian attack, the matter was handled with kid gloves: the word "neurosis" proved that the authors were *a priori* excluding the pseudo-neurotic manifestations (which in reality are psychotic) of obsessions/compulsions. It was only in *DSM-IV*, in 1994, when "neurosis" disappeared for good, that the need was felt for a new criterion to compensate for the lost distinction. So, we read, we must take into account the *insight* of the obsessed, and establish that they are not absolutely convinced of the necessity to accomplish their rituals. Thus, a difference had to be established between obsessions and "over-valued ideas" (OVI), and even delusional ideas. *DSM-III* still kept one foot in a world where Anna Freud's distinction between obsessional neurosis and psychosis with obsessional symptoms remained in evidence – even for the rather large number of people who no longer believed in psychoanalysis. So, the real break came in the 1990s.

§1. The two crucial problems of the definition of OCD in DSM

How are obsessions and compulsions articulated with each other? *DSM-III* deemed it necessary to clarify this: compulsions were a "response" to obsessions. This is a remarkable formulation, and there are two ways in which it can be understood. Either we believe that obsessions *cause* anxiety, and compulsions relieve it; or that obsessions are the *reason* for compulsions, which would explain why these compulsions have an aim that they seek to attain, if necessary through repetition. Each of these readings has its advantages and its disadvantages. Let us take the causal reading. It brings obsessions/compulsions and phobias closer together, as if ritualising were a sort of reflex action the instant one becomes obsessed with an idea. Here, anxiety is clearly a prime mover, and compulsion a means of discharging it. But how can we account for the intentionality of this discharge, which is not purely a movement of avoidance but a ritual? And where has it ever been seen that flight reflexes are repeated *ad infinitum* and seek to achieve perfect accomplishment? Take the rationalist reading. It explains everything the causal reading fails to justify: the intentionality of the ritual, and the meaning of the obsession. But beyond the fact that a supplementary causal factor is needed in order to explain why the obsession "passes into action" in a compulsive fashion (a body will not be moved by one reason alone), obsession is still a really bizarre "reason" – a reason whose absurdity seriously compromises the status of reason itself.

Let us linger on this last point. Why is it so awkward to maintain that compulsions are intentional actions that "respond" to an obsession, which is their reason, unless this reason is absurd? Because this is where we see the price that has been paid for abandoning the Freudian position, which linked obsessions to a fantasy, whose diverse actualisations, in dreams, in jokes, and finally in *Zwangsvorstellungen* (obsessional ideas) in the strict sense, *relativised* the irrationality of any particular obsession and any particular isolated compulsion. Because this fantasy is a dense network of representations, images, memories, and symbols, which tell a kind of story. For Freud, it was even a characteristic of the obsessional to find each and every one of his own compulsions or obsessions absurd, when taken separately; because in isolating them from one another, he creates a defence against the fantasy of (oedipal) desire which is their cause. Even more clear-cut is Lacan's idea, according to which the relation between obsessions and compulsions is conceived as a structured "myth" (which an individual forges in order to spare him- or herself anxiety and guilt) with a "ritual", the successive executions of which refer to each other, and all of them refer to the myth (so these are not just disjointed episodes of motor activity, needing to be started again from zero each time). In contrast to the mass of difficulties encountered in trying to adjust the absurd ideas of patients and their compulsive "response", Freud's and Lacan's propositions begin to seem quite attractive again. Methodologically speaking, indeed, the holistic approaches have not had a good press. But, in the case in point, wishing to avoid them at all costs means there is a risk of destroying the very object of our study. *DSM-III* lists the compulsions that are statistically the most frequent: checking, washing, touching, etc. But these gestures, isolated from any scenario they might form part of, and even from any description of their function in the patients' behaviour, are *no longer even actions.* How can they be distinguished from straightforward automatisms with a neurological basis? We need another stipulative clause: they are compulsions... on the express condition that they are neither stereotypical behaviours nor the effects of a cerebral lesion! All of this is so utterly *ad hoc.*

Along with these impasses, we can observe the problem of a purely stipulative definition of compulsions and obsessions. Such a definition implies that one could just ignore the ordinary usage of terms that express the intrinsically problematic nature of human action. It treats such words with suspicion, as if it were impossible to clarify them and as if the interplay of their reciprocal articulations, which is certainly very subtle, had no value whatsoever – whereas it is precisely this interplay we live with, and it is the locus of the question of the malaise we are claiming to elucidate. In *Âmes scrupuleuses, vies d'angoisse, tristes obsédés*, I proposed a characterisation of obsessions/compulsions which sanctions speaking about them in ordinary ways (Castel, 2012, p. 423). When it is impossible to prevent our thoughts and desires from aiming at a certain object or state of things, precisely because it is something we do not want, and we do not even want to think about it – well, that is exactly the point where we realise we are obsessed with it. We think about it "compulsively" and we are "obsessed" by an attraction we push away[8]. Thus, we are caught between an "absolutely not" that insists in the mind, and an "in spite of oneself", which seeks furiously, against our will, to commit the act. This ordinary grammar of obsession and acting against our will is entirely liquidated by the stipulative style of *DSM*. What constituted the incapacity to act here becomes the principle of the mutual engagement of two cogs, intellectual obsessions and gestural compulsions. There is no mistake in this. The *grammatical* solidarity of obsessions and compulsions, which was still taken for granted in the experience of self-inflicted constraint, has been deliberately destroyed in order to enable the search for an *empirical* connection between the two.

Trying to escape this hornets' nest, *DSM-IV,* in 1994, preferred to neutralise any opportunities for contradiction. Cause or reason, it does not really matter. Yes, there are people who *think* they "respond" to their obsessions by performing rituals, and even a number of them who *feel* that their compulsions relieve their anxiety. But all this is subjective; it is not an essential property of OCD. I will come back to this, but one thing is clear. *DSM-IV clearly had both feet in a new moral universe.* Lived experience still counted for something. But in contrast to what had still appeared in *DSM-III*, it was now possibly just a side issue. Now it was preferable to focus on the mechanisms of the brain on the one hand, which certainly "cause" this subjective sensation (here we find ourselves right in the midst of the "decade of the brain") and, on the other hand, we must not leave by the wayside the considerable number of patients for whom the "intrapsychic" articulation of obsessions and compulsions no longer made any sense. The 1990s were not the 1980s, either at the epistemological or the sociological level.

The best indicator of this shift, which is highlighted so clearly by the psychopathology of OCD, but which is also perceptible in subtle reconfigurations of the sense of self, is the weight accorded, or not, to the "subjective resistance" to obsessions/compulsions.

DSM-III distinguished OCD from the "compulsive personality" (301.40, the good old anal character) by defining the former as an "ego-dystonic" experience and the latter as an "ego-syntonic" experience. No one ever took the risk of defining those terms. They were supposed to be self-explanatory. But they point to an intrinsic difficulty. The idea of a subjective resistance to obsessional ideas and to rituals made for a strong connection between the description of OCD in *DSM-III* and the traditional phenomenology of the illness. For a whole generation of psychiatrists, speaking of obsessions and compulsions without referring to this struggle meant speaking about nothing at all. Qualifying OCD as ego-dystonic had an echo of the old concept of intrapsychic conflict, while avoiding Freudian terminology. Above all, in accordance with the postulate of an a-theoretical description as starting point, one avoided imputing any causal role to this conflict.

This was to change completely, beginning as early as the 1990s with the publication of *DSM-IV*. In my view, there were three contributory factors.

1. The first was the clinical evidence that children do not always "struggle" with obsessions/compulsions. The younger they are, the less this is the case. Would it then be true to say that children's OCD, which has all the formal traits of adult OCD, *minus* subjective resistance, and which is treated with the same psychotropic medication, and which in any case develops into OCD *with* resistance, is not actually already OCD? That would be a bit far-fetched. Nevertheless, I might add, the only way to treat them is to *create* this conflict where there was none. The cognitive-behavioural therapists are unanimous on this score. Children only fight against OCD symptoms that they consider to be their enemies. We even find retrospective reflections by young patients who have been cured, who wish they could have their symptoms back, because fighting against them had given meaning to their lives (Vera, 2004, p. 184)! As we can see, intrapsychic conflict, having been chased out of theory via the door, finds its way back in through the window of the clinic.

2. The second factor is even more worrying. A number of obsessional adults do not experience the so-called internal resistance either – which does not mean that their OCD is ego-syntonic, or that these are clearly cases of psychosis. Their malaise no longer expresses itself in the register of conflict! It speaks for itself that many of these observations were reported by obsessionals who were themselves medical practitioners, and even specialists in the treatment of OCD, people who had thereby become sensitive to the nuances which seemed to escape clinicians who were not themselves obsessional. The following was reported by Ian Osborn, founder of group therapy for obsessive-compulsive disorder, and celebrated author of *Tormenting Thoughts and Secret Rituals: the hidden epidemic of obsessive-compulsive disorder*:

> In individual therapy I can encourage people to take control, to stand up to OCD, but the response is often minimal. Hearing

those who speak out of personal experience is infinitely more powerful. A truck driver suffering obsessions that his shoes were full of fleas and mites scrubbed his feet nightly with alcohol, which left them painfully cracked and fissured. Even though it was obvious to him that his compulsive washing was irrational, he told our group that it had simply never occurred to him that he could resist it. He had just assumed that if he did so something terrible would happen. Once encouraged to take control of his rituals, he made surprisingly quick progress. After one month he was able to go a whole week without scrubbing. He reported to the group that as soon as his obsessions would begin, he just said to himself, "To hell with those obsessions; I'm not going to start that washing." (Osborn, 1998, p. 123)

It matters little that a Freudian might see this as a case of psychosis. It suffices that it does not qualify as such within the new paradigm for the entire body of evidence to be annulled that had been re-affirmed over the years regarding the internal resistance of individual subjects to obsessions/compulsions. It is also the consequence of the stipulative nature of the definitions of *DSM*. If one of the clauses does not fit, it is child's play to exclude it. Because they are constructed in the form of a Philonian implication: if a symptom is obsessional, then it has such and such properties. Hence, we can see that if the property of resistance is missing, then the symptom is not obsessional. But the rule of construction of these definitions, via the conversion of *modus ponens* to *modus tollens*, ensures that it is possible to make them say the opposite. It was established that people who did not resist were obsessionals. So the definition of OCD had to be changed, and from then on, what had previously been a criterion for exclusion now allowed the definition to be extended to include those who had previously been excluded. No empirical discovery, no clinical progress: just a new convention. Thanks to this formal sleight of hand, which once again was made possible by the stipulative nature of the definitions in *DSM*, the internal resistance of obsessionals, which had always been a sufficient condition for the diagnosis of OCD, was no longer a necessary one.

3. The third factor concerns the acceptable means of complaining in any given era. Of all the factors involved in the liquidation of the vocabulary of intrapsychic conflict, this is the most powerful.

The little gimmicks of redefinition in *DSM* are subordinate to it. Again, Osborn is a precious example of this trend. He no longer locates the state of being conflicted, which is so massively present in other cases of OCD, in the person. Each individual explains their conflicts by attributing them to whatever they wish. It might be to Satan, if they like; that has just as much value as psychoanalytic hypotheses (ibid., 1998, p. 163). For Osborn, the place where conflict really takes place is in the brain. Because "an obsession is a struggle between a part of the brain that wants to dismiss an unacceptable thought from consciousness and another part that wants to process it further" (ibid., p. 167). For many people, the idea that the brain can "be in conflict with itself" is at the very best a metaphor. Only human beings can, in the real sense, have conflicts with themselves, not their body parts. Osborn's formulation is truly mind-boggling. According to him, I could "fight with myself" by hitting my right hand with my left! But here, obviously, *we are no longer dealing with metaphor.* The conflict is intra-cerebral *in the real sense.* Perhaps we should even go as far as rectifying the way we use ordinary language to verify empirically whether our psychical experiences of conflict are rooted in conflicts between our cerebral sub-systems or not ...

Without our realising it, here we are, having left behind the objective psychiatry of OCD in favour of considerations of the great social categories of the perception of the self.

§2. From a stipulative definition to a normative definition: patients' associations enter the stage

It is hardly surprising. Between *DSM-III* and *DSM-IIIR*, between the beginning and the end of the 1980s, a phenomenon occurred which had unforeseen consequences: the emergence of the first associations of patients who recognised themselves in relation to the new taxonomy. In the United States, the Obsessive-Compulsive Foundation was set up in 1986, and among the young psychiatrists who supported it, we can find a number of the major physicians who would go on to publish the more frequently cited studies on OCD. In Great Britain, Triumph Over Phobia (which included OCD sufferers as well) was founded in 1987. The media soon began to take an interest in this epidemic. In March 1987, at the instigation of the Obsessive-Compulsive Foundation, "20–20", a popular programme on the television network ABC, made a broadcast on this theme. Tens of thousands of people discovered that they were suffering from an illness that officially existed, and which had precise criteria that were publicly available. However, *DSM-III* did not give any criteria of severity, and as I have already indicated, the essential feature of these "new" obsessionals who were now being counted in by the epidemiologists was that they were subclinical cases of moderate severity. They were easier to treat, and therefore became the target group for the new therapies which were looking for a market. In 1987, fluoxetine was launched onto the market under the name of Prozac®, with enormous success. Its anti-obsessional properties had already been recognised for two years, and it was all the more rapidly exploited because the molecule of reference, clomipramine, quite bizarrely, did not receive authorisation for the treatment of OCD in the United States until 1989. From 1990 onwards, therapists were overwhelmed by the number of patients who sought their help: the epidemiological promise of an explosion of cases finally materialised in the hospitals. This allowed the first cohort studies to be set up with an adequate statistical basis. And since patients were concomitantly benefiting from the new psychotropic medications and forms of cognitive therapy that were less unpleasant than the austere behavioural regimes standardised in London in the 1970s, there were more and more positive results – in patients who twenty years earlier would have been highly unlikely to receive a diagnosis of obsessional neurosis.

Even the specialists remained quite reserved about all this. In spite of the advantages of the situation for furthering their careers, they were not unaware of the danger that a less than rigorous definition of OCD would pose to their attempt to discover, for the first time in the history of psychiatry, the aetiology of a major mental illness. We can go even further and say that as they were forced to adopt the criteria of *DSM-III* in order to operationalise the recruitment of cohorts (for epidemiological purposes, for clinical trials, for comparative studies between rival therapies, and later for genetic studies), many found that those criteria plainly contradicted the hypotheses of their research. I shall explain why (see §3). Therefore, they tended to raise the thresholds for inclusion. It appears that in field studies prior to the publication of *DSM-IIIR*, and even more so in those from the period before the publication of *DSM-IV*, the patients identified as obsessional were more severely ill than those covered by the Five-city study.

But this restrictive movement could not stand up to a social dynamic that was moving in completely the opposite direction. The afflicted members of the public had not read the *DSM* criteria as stipulative definitions which were neither true nor false, but merely useful for the purposes of classification. On the contrary, they saw these definitions as being *normative*: "what you needed to have" in order to be obsessional/compulsive; and notably, to define the conditions for legitimate recruitment to a militant patients' association aiming to make the public authorities acknowledge their morbidity, so that they could claim reimbursement for their treatment and promote research into their pathology.

OCD and the new therapies for OCD were therefore co-constructed in a way that enabled a completely new audience to find recognition in the tables of obsessions/compulsions published in *DSM*: people who found they could locate their subclinical maladies there (which is not in the least to underestimate their suffering!), but also people who were no longer lumbered with the classic condition of the "internal struggle", in other words, with the profound moral subjectivation of the intra-psychical conflict, and lastly, for the same reasons, people who were completely open to the idea that the intrusive thoughts and affects that disturbed them could have a non-subjective cause – for example, a cerebral cause.

The generalisation of psychometric instruments has to be understood in this context, in which a trend among researchers to restrict OCD to the most severe cases met with an opposing trend among the patients' associations, where the spectrum of OCD was broadened to legitimise less severe and less specific cases. Because these psychometric instruments could serve both the one and the other trend. The Leyton obsessional inventory, which was mobilised for the Five-city study of OCD, had its imitators. The Maudsley group put forward another inventory in 1977. The Padua inventory came out in 1988. By 2012 there were at least half a dozen questionnaires online that you could fill in yourself to find out if you were obsessional/compulsive or not (Hodgson & Rachman, 1977; Sanavio, 1988). As a complementary development in the field of measures of severity, which was indispensable in order to set the thresholds for inclusion in the studies, a tool was rapidly imposed on researchers. In 1989, Wayne C. Goodman, who three years earlier had played a role in setting up the Obsessive-Compulsive Foundation, published a scale in the *Archives of General Psychiatry* which was universally successful: the Yale-Brown Obsessive-Compulsive Scale (Y-BOCS) (Goodman, Price, Rasmussen, Mazue, Fleischmann, Hill, Heninger, & Charney, 1989).

All of these tools are double-edged. They enable people to identify themselves as patients. They also enable them to identify the nature of their symptoms as stable and impersonal, so that they can themselves objectify what they are suffering from and distance themselves from the more or less bizarre story they tell themselves. The Y-BOCS, which nowadays is administered routinely, as much in clinical trials as in office-based practice, is just as suitable for the evaluation of the effects of medication. It is divided into two sub-scales, one for obsessions and the other for compulsions (which means they can be adjusted to the *DSM* criteria). In each sub-scale five questions are asked, about time occupied by obsessional thoughts/compulsive behaviours, level of interference on a daily basis, level of distress experienced, "subjective resistance", and degree of control over symptoms. Each item is scored from zero to four. A score of sixteen or less is graded as "mild" OCD. The minimum required for a therapy to be considered effective is a reduction of at least twenty-five per cent on the Y-BOCS scale. But obviously it is sufficient to score twelve with three items rated at four, such as spending eight hours a day checking everything, under the cosh of incessant doubt, and to feel absolutely terrible throughout the process, to create a portrait of someone who would find it hard to deny he was extremely unwell.

Cognitive therapists do not like the Y-BOCS at all. Because while it allows the effects of psychotropic medication to be evaluated, it is far less useful in measuring subjective experience. Paul M. Salkovskis, the British psychologist who had so much influence on cognitive therapies for OCD, noted that not only does the Y-BOCS fail to measure avoidance, which is a decisive parameter in the psychotherapy of this kind of disorder, but it also instils further doubt in the subjects of the investigation, by asking them about the degree of "control" they have gained over their obsessions and compulsions. Well, says Salkovskis, a successful therapy is a therapy during which patients manage to stop asking themselves questions about control! One could generalise here. Because the question of self-mastery is omnipresent in these questionnaires and scales. These tools in themselves show a substantial affinity with OCD. They encourage patients to "rationalise", to "objectivise", and ultimately, to de-moralise their experience. Thus, they measure pathology, but at the same time they crystallise it. Hence, we start hearing of seasoned therapists emphasising the danger that patients can transfer the responsibility for their progress either to the practitioner or to the method he uses. They fetishise the reduction of scores, and like detached spectators or even robots, obey the instructions that are supposed to lower the scores.

Be that as it may, these inventories of typical obsessions/compulsions, such as the Y-BOCS, standardise not only the illness but also the patients. The inventories extract abstract narrative segments from the complex scenarios of obsessionals ("fear of contracting a horrible illness", "concerns about clothing", "rituals of opening the eyes wide or of blinking", "beliefs that certain numbers bring good or bad luck", etc.). But just using these typical symptoms, could we not compose an infinite number of life stories? The "typical symptoms" are the result of the pulverisation of a thousand concrete existences into a grainy dust of de-contextualised instances. But that does not matter very much. Because this is the fundamental condition for the statistical analysis of clinical results. Since the end of the 1970s, descriptions of *individualised* clinical states before, during and after treatment have totally disappeared from the literature. They have been replaced by measures of effectiveness or by the use of mean scores. Hence, there is a sense that they are justifying *the fact* of having used such and such a treatment, by measuring *how much* the patients have progressed, and they are forgetting to take into account *what* was actually being treated, and *in whom*. Everyone is happy: the researchers, because they are measuring an objective and trans-individual phenomenon; and the patients, especially those who belong to associations, and who provide the bulk of the cohorts, because the impersonality of these practices is consonant with the idea that each and every person is the victim of a malady which is just as real, and just as external, as diabetes. The uniformity of the techniques and of the measurements allows comparisons to be made, and a biological basis of OCD to be sought. It also satisfies the democratic idea that everyone has the right to a treatment that is equally objective, or at least equally objectively validated as the one my neighbour and fellow-sufferer is receiving. This harmony confers its dual social and epistemological strength on the system: it is a formidable machine which works away silently, but at full power, in the very depths of contemporary moral life. To criticise it would be frankly unwise.

Anyway, this conciliation of social and epistemological interests in the de-moralisation of the lived experience of the obsessional is only one part of the story. Because this double standardisation applied respectively to patients and illnesses has coincided with the triumph of a hypothesis which is extremely audacious, and which requires a completely different reading of the epidemiological explosion of OCD, and of the justification of the definitions in *DSM*.

§3. How we all became "normal" obsessionals

There is in fact a second way of accounting for the fact that so many people, at one time or another during their lives, will experience obsessions and compulsions. Because their newly-established epidemiological commonplaceness proves, not that they are both pathological and extremely widespread but, on the contrary, that they are normal or generally sub-clinical. There are, then, obsessions that are "normal", present in an enormous number of people, possibly in everyone, and which correspond to the *DSM* criteria, but the actual problem is to understand why, in that case, not everyone becomes as ill as the "real" obsessionals/compulsives. Well into the 2000s, this hypothesis has appeared to be the true path for science. It was the subject of an almost unanimous consensus among cognitive-behavioural therapists.

So, we are all obsessives? Is this the homage paid by scientific psychiatry to the universal inhibition of action of the historians and anthropologists? Not at all.

The concept of "normal" obsessions/compulsions never led to the idea of a social or cultural regularity in the phenomena of internal constraint. On the contrary: it set in motion the process of their naturalisation, their anti-historical embedding into biological and ethological regularities, which reinforced the de-contextualisation of individual case histories.

To adopt this hypothesis is to take the side of integrating the dimensionality intrinsic to the Y-BOCS into the categorical criteria of *DSM* (the criteria for OCD on axis II). But there is more to it than that. Because how can a normal obsession become pathological, other than by scoring high on the Y-BOCS? It is through the way people "assume" these obsessions, about which they then make themselves feel anxious and guilty. It suffices to look at the reflexive pronouns: "They make themselves anxious, they blame themselves." This is the great return of the *self* in OCD, as the causal principle that is responsible for the morbid effect of obsessions which should have remained "normal". Because nobody falls ill simply because they have obsessions, but rather because of the *way* in which they "obsess" about their obsessions. There is thus an element of responsibility in the way one "assumes" obsessions. Guilt, however, is not involved; it is dissipated once one has learnt how to "deal differently with" obsessions. Once this capacity has been acquired, one can just leave them be, like any normal phenomena, with no further reason to make oneself feel guilty or anxious about them. All that remains is, if I may say so, a layman's responsibility: it circumscribes a sphere of self-manipulation within which, through procedures I shall now describe, one manages cleverly to rid oneself of what had been troublesome. In this case, the self is an internal system, and it is possible to optimise its performance. It must be grasped firmly like a mental thing that obeys certain laws. This mental thing is ultimately presumed to regulate its own guilt and anxiety, its moral and social affects.

What is the basis of the notion of "normal" obsession? In what follows, Jakes (1996, p. 10f) sums up the examples that form the basis of his main arguments of defence, and I shall expand on his critique:

> Rachman and Parkinson (1981) present the following anxious thoughts (among others), all of which were reported by mothers concerning their children who were at the time in hospital for surgery: "Ever since I knew she was booked in I have been thinking what might go wrong with the anaesthetic and surgery." (The same mother is reported as having a "repetitive image" in which "I have seen her lying there like a vegetable and not coming round from the operation".) "I have this repeated image of K. on a trolley, and they put him in a bed and then I see the blood everywhere. I try hard to clear it from my mind. The image frightens the life out of me." "It's been on my mind the whole time. I haven't been able to stop myself thinking about him and his operation." "I was thinking about it all the time. I was constantly going through in my mind how I would explain things to him. I keep seeing him in his gown, asleep, being taken down the theatre. I've seen him go down in my mind." "I keep hearing him and seeing him in hospital, crying." (All quotes from Rachman and Parkinson, 1981, pp. 115, 117.)

Granted, these mothers' reactions are "normal". It would be most peculiar if they did not feel worried. These obsessions would become "pathological" if the anticipation of the risk became so absurd that, for example, the mothers refused to allow their children to be operated on, even though they could be persuaded that this was irrational; or if they felt "guilty in advance" for an accident in the operating theatre; or if they feared that the accident would happen because they were thinking about it ("magical thinking"). They may not have reached this point, but they find themselves playing with the idea that *they are almost there*, as if the path that stretched from the *o* of a determined quantity, and from there to infinity, was already completely traced out. Therefore, there are "normal" obsessions, which are the degree-*o* of obsessionality, which have all the traits of obsessions, except that they are not "pathological".

Why would we accept this? To start with, it is false to say that obsessions are commonplace. It is possible to describe them in a way that makes them sound commonplace, but that is quite different. In this case, the means of making them sound commonplace is *ad hoc*: it consists in saying that mothers who have those thoughts "are not making them into" marked obsessions. But what one wants to prove is quite another matter: the same examples were also used to demonstrate that these women had come close to doing just that. You can't have your cake and eat it. They make an obsession sound commonplace so that it remains "normal" on the one hand, and then, once the normal obsession has been established in this way, find it marvellous that it has not crossed a pathological threshold, and start looking for a "cognitive mechanism" that has immunised the mothers. A further objection is as follows: two fundamental characteristics are missing from these quasi-obsessions. First of all, they are not absurd. Indeed, they are entirely understandable – and by the mothers as well, who are not remotely disturbed by having such thoughts. To be more precise, these mothers are disturbed by the *content* of their thoughts, but not by the *form* taken by the thoughts. It pains them to think *of that*, but not to think of it *like that*. Where is the feeling of intrusion? In what sense are these "normal" obsessions perceived as being strange psychical elements? The same goes for all the other "normal" obsessions found in the literature: thinking of pushing someone under a train in the underground when one is hemmed in on a crowded platform; shouting out in the middle of a solemn silence, etc., which have certainly gone through the minds of a good number of people. If we think like this, why should there not also be "normal" traumatic thoughts, for example when I think or dream involuntarily and repetitively of disasters I have witnessed, but without sweating, without feeling anxious, without the visual intensity of my memories disturbing me? If I have all of the mental content of the traumatised person, without feeling the effect these images impose on me, who is to say that I am traumatised? Well, let us return to *DSM-IIIR*: are these so-called obsessional ideas accompanied by a feeling that I have to "respond" to them with rituals? Not at all. By the way, Rachman and Parkinson insist on the morbid *image* that occurs in the mothers, but do not raise the question of the *acts* that might be motivated by these obsessions. There are no impulses to rush to the clinic and stop everything, for example, nor any superstitious gestures.[9] We have to make up our minds about this. These re-descriptions cannot "normalise" obsessions/compulsions, because as soon as they occur, their criteria for identification as OCD evaporate.

But by its fruits shall ye know the tree. What if the idea of "normal" obsession enabled new fields of research to be opened up? At the time of writing (2012), this is the direction taken by *DSM-V*. "Normal" obsessions have now gained the right to be included, because dimensions had to be added to the categories; in other words, each symptom had to be broadened out into a continuum, from the mildest forms to the most severe. At the same time, it is an opportunity for research into more and more discreet signs of the illness (*soft signs*, as the neurologists call them), which is in perfect accord with the progressive cerebralisation of OCD (Hollander, 2011; Leckman, et al, 2010).

At the same time, after all the hesitations around its "scientific" and post-Freudian characterisation, OCD seems to be hanging in a void. "Subjective resistance", which had been a core concept throughout a century of psychiatry, is no longer deemed a necessary condition for the disorder, let alone a sufficient one; and what is more, its pathological character has to be justified, since the simple fact of being obsessed is no longer necessarily abnormal. As Jakes puts it so well, the various sub-types of OCD are only very loosely related members of the same family; there are so many different versions, so many different modalities and intensities: from the most ethical forms, i.e., the traditional obsessions/compulsions, to the most neurological forms, which border on stereotypy. To this I will add that it could not be otherwise, because the way of life in which they were interwoven in a thousand practical and perceptible ways, both moral and cultural, is gradually disappearing. I would even go so far as to say that without the list of typical examples drawn from the glorious history of the illness, and without the federalising negation of the clinical heritage of psychoanalysis, there would be no means of arriving at a mutual understanding of the very thing we are talking about. And furthermore, we have lost the sense of what sort of vision of the self the old experience of self-constraint was attached to. The notion of internal conflict no longer fits the bill. For all that, the new self that is susceptible to becoming obsessed has yet to find an incontestable centre of gravity.

Notes

1. In the sections preceding the present chapter of his book *La fin des coupables* (2012) Castel had outlined and discussed the history of obsessions, guilt, and anxiety and how they acquired different status in different historical eras, culminating in the emergence of the "post-guilty beings" at our present age. In the chapter presented here references to earlier sections in this book have been added with the author's permission when it seemed helpful for an understanding of the text. [Ed.]

2. See the work of Norbert Elias on the increasing demand for intensification of "*Selbstzwang*" (self-constraint) in "civilising processes" (Elias, 1939). Mark the equivocation inherent in the German term: *Selbstzwang* means both self-constraint and constraint for anyone to become a self. This equivocation informs the whole Eliasian project of tracing back the psychological and moral dimension of the rise of the individual in the historical metamorphoses of the feeling of inner constraint/restraint (obsessions, scruples, etc.).

3. The nuns of Loudun, Kierkegaard, and Freud are main characters Castel examines in previous sections of his book *La fin des coupables* (2012).

4. Most recently, obsessions have begun to appear which can be deduced from these things: polluting, wasting energy, even (can we believe our eyes?) failing to optimise your "carbon footprint" (Jones, Wootton, Vaccaro & Menzies, 2012)

5. These costs have apparently increased five-fold. At the end of the 1990s, it was costing around $1500 per patient per year. Today (2012) in the United States, it is estimated that cognitive-behavioural therapy costs $3000 (at least twenty sessions at $150) and psychotropic medication costs $4500 per year (Franklin, 2005, p. 378).

6. The cooperation between Robins and the architect-in-chief of *DSM-III*, Robert L. Spitzer, is a major event in the history of psychiatry: if they had not met and collaborated, the idea of defining mental illnesses both clinically and statistically would never have been conceived. The definitions of symptoms utilised by these researchers were in fact those that had already been operationalised for the purposes of the manual. On the other hand, the *DSM-III* criteria for exclusion were not taken into account, in order better to skew the results of co-morbidity in the general population.

7. For a useful critical summary see Demazeux, 2013.

8. In contemporary English, *compulsive* can be applied to thinking processes and *obsessive* to gestures and actions. There is nothing natural about this medical dichotomy. This has led to certain equivocations which, in my view, have made it difficult to rediscover certain facts that had been known for a very long time, such as "tics" that were not physical, but mental.

9. Work has been published on the subject of "normal" compulsions. But they are liable to the same refutations: there is a sophistical shift from the *content* of compulsive actions which are supposedly "normal", to the *form* of these actions which runs counter to the volition of the subject (Muris, Merckelbach, & Clavan, 1997).

References

Castel, P.-H. (2012). *Âmes scrupuleuses, vies d'angoisse, tristes obsédés. Vol. I.* Paris: Ithaque

Cooper, J. E. (1970). The Leyton obsessional inventory. *Psychological Medicine*, 1: 48–64.

Cottraux, J. (1998). *Les Ennemis intérieurs: Obsessions et compulsions.* Paris: Odile Jacob.

Demazeux, S. (2013). *Pourquoi les DSM? Compter et classer dans la psychiatrie américaine.* Paris: Ithaque.

Elias, N. (1939). *The Civilizing Process.* E. Dunning, J. Goudsblom, & S. Mennell (Eds.), E. F. N. Jephcott (Trans.). Oxford: Blackwell, 2000.

Franklin, M. E. (2005). Combining serotonin medication with cognitive-behavior therapy: Is it necessary for all OCD patients? In: J. S. Abramowitz, & A. C. Houts (Eds.), *Concepts and Controversies in Obsessive-Compulsive Disorder.* New York: Springer, 2005, pp. 377–391.

Goodman, W. K., Price, L. H., Rasmussen, S. A., Mazure, C., Fleischmann, R. L., Hill, C. L., Heninger, G. R., & Charney, D. S. (1989). The Yale-Brown

Obsessive Compulsive Scale. I. Development, use, and reliability. *Archives of General Psychiatry, 46 (11)*: 1006–11.

Hodgson, R. J. & Rachman, S. J. (1977). Obsessional-Compulsive Complaints. *Behaviour Research and Therapy, 15*: 389–395.

Hollander, E. (2011). Obsessive-Compulsive Spectrum Disorders: Refining the Research Agenda for DSM-V. *American Psychiatric Association*. Washington, DC and London: American Psychiatric Publishing.

Jakes, I. (1996). *Theoretical Approaches to Obsessive-Compulsive Disorder*. Cambridge: Cambridge University Press.

Janet, P. (1926). *De l'Angoisse à l'extase: Étude sur les croyances et les sentiments. (Un délire religieux. La croyance)*. Paris: Alcan.

Jones M. K., Wootton B. M., Vaccaro L. D., & Menzies R. G. (2012). The impact of climate change on obsessive compulsive checking concerns. *Australasian and New Zealand Journal of Psychiatry, 46*: 183–184.

Karno M., Golding J. M., Sorenson S. B., & Burnam M. A. (1988). The epidemiology of obsessive-compulsive disorder in five US communities. *Archives of General Psychiatry 45*: 1094–1099.

Lacan, J. (1950/2008). Lettre inédite à Marie de la Trinité, 19 septembre 1950. *Le Nouvel Âne, 8*: 14.

Lasch, C. (1979). *The Culture of Narcissism: American Life in an Age of Diminishing Expectations*. New York: Norton.

Leckman, J. F., Denys, D., Simpson, H. B., Mataix-Cols, D., Hollander, E., Saxena, S., Miguel, E. C., Rauch, S. L., Goodman, W. K., Phillips, K. A., & Stein, D. J. (2010). Obsessive-Compulsive Disorder: A Review of the Diagnostic Criteria and Possible Subtype and Dimensional Specifiers for DSM-V. *Depression and Anxiety, 27*: 507–527.

Muris, P., Merckelbach, H., & Clavan, M. (1997). Abnormal and normal compulsions. *Behaviour Research and Therapy 35 (3)*: 249–52.

Osborn, I. (1998). *Tormenting Thoughts and Secret Rituals. The Hidden Epidemic of Obsessive-Compusive Disorders*. New York: Dell.

Rachman, S. J. & Parkinson, L. (1981). Unwanted intrusive cognitions. *Advances in Behaviour Research and Therapy, 3*: 89–123.

Sanavio, E. (1988). Obsessions and compulsions: The Padua Inventory. *Behaviour Research and Therapy, 26 (2)*: 169–177.

Sennet, R. (2006). *The Culture of the New Capitalism*. New Haven: Yale.

Vera, L. (2004). *Troubles obsessionnels compulsifs chez l'enfant et l'adolescent*. Paris: Dunod.

CHAPTER TWO

Lacanian approaches to obsession

DARIAN LEADER

Psychoanalytic conceptualisation of obsessional neurosis since at least the late 1950s seems strangely stunted. After Freud's classic papers and the contributions of Alexander, Bergler, Deutsch, Glover, Jones, and Rado, there are many published case reports yet very little that advances the theorisation of obsessional structure. Lacan's commentaries from the early 1950s to the seminar on transference in 1961 (Lacan, 1960–1961) provide powerful revisions of Freud's perspectives, yet today they risk being reduced to glib aphorisms such as "Am I alive or dead?" or "The obsessional denies the desire of the Other". In Lacanian studies, obsessional neurosis is rarely explored beyond such formulae, mimicking the reliance on verbal incantations which is so ubiquitous in obsession itself.

How could we explain this apparent neglect of what had certainly been a central clinical structure for Freud? There are two immediate answers to this question. First, it is possible that the elegance and clarity of Freud's – and then Lacan's – account of the phenomenology and structure of obsession were deemed sufficient. If all was explained, there was no urgency for further research. Second, the subsuming of obsessional neurosis into the later category of obsessive-compulsive disorder (OCD) operated a shift from questions of structure to surface features. And with this displacement came a weakening and a confusion of nosological issues.

OCD brought together a number of symptomatic features that are, in effect, trans-structural: doubt, ritualisation, intrusive thoughts and images, contamination fears, and a seemingly reduced affective range may all be found in obsession but equally so in psychosis. The new label of OCD made phenomena such as these constitutive of a diagnostic category rather than seeing them as clues which would require further investigation as to the diagnosis. This meant that diagnostic questions became lost in both mainstream psychiatry and in many psychoanalytic currents outside the Lacanian orientation.

The creation of the category of OCD is telling here. Nosological histories are notoriously imprecise, as if the actual moment when OCD separated off from obsession cannot be pinpointed. This echoes the chronological opacity that is one of the most well-known phenomena of obsession: the temporal coordinate of a change in behaviour or some crucial event in the subject's past is either left continuously vague or is shifted around defensively. Similarly, the term OCD itself has the structure of a symptom. Where the British tended to translate *Zwangsvorstellung* as *obsession*, the Americans preferred *compulsion* (Rado, 1959). Unable to choose, the new diagnostic label retained both, illustrating exactly the Freudian explanation of the obsessional symptom: faced with the impossibility of deciding between two alternatives, the subject keeps both, at a price.

***

This is indeed a useful place to start if we wish to differentiate obsessional neurosis as such from other structures which use obsessional symptomology. When someone complains of an "obsession" or "compulsion", its exact form – what Freud called its "wording" (*Wortlaut*) – must be made precise. Many people might have a compulsion to make sure the stove is turned off when they leave the house, with thoughts of an impending catastrophe. Repeated attempts will be made to verify this, ranging from returning home to taking serial photographs of the dials before leaving. In itself, this is a common phenomenon of both obsessional neurosis and of schizophrenia, and hence the importance of establishing its function.

In schizophrenia, such compulsions may index the porosity of the body and the subject's attempts to generate a barrier to protect it.

Demarcations between spaces are cardinal here, and compulsions may serve to maintain a division between inside and outside that is fundamentally unstable. In obsession, however, if the underlying thought process is elicited, it tends to display a conditional form: if the stove isn't turned off, then harm will befall a loved one. And, crucially, if for the schizophrenic subject what matters may be knowing that the stove is turned off, a key element of the symptom in obsession is the actual wish to resist the feeling of compulsion. This is the problem of 'will' that nineteenth century alienists saw as central to obsession.

Adding to this potential for diagnostic confusion is the clinical fact that when someone presents with a classical picture of obsessional neurosis, with pervasive doubt, ceremonials, and verbal intrusion, the correct diagnosis is most often schizophrenia. This is because the repertoire of obsessional symptomology is being used to limit and absorb an invasive libidinal danger. Threatened both psychically and physically, the subject appeals to the defences most readily available, which are those associated with the structure of language itself: binary oppositions, links between words and the material isolation of words themselves. Obsessional symptomology is, after all, intrinsically bound up with the fabric of language. When a subject uses this to defend him or herself, it is a mistake to then automatically assume that the structure is obsessional neurosis.

Similarly, the very clarity of the obsessional phenomena may suggest psychosis, since obsessional subjects often keep their rituals and compulsions secret, or simply have no need to speak about them as they are not experienced as symptoms. Hence the way in which rituals associated not just with toilet habits or masturbation but with leaving the house or crossing thresholds may only come to light years into an analysis, whereas they may be discussed relatively soon after interviews begin for a psychotic subject as they involve the urgency of a day to day defence which may collapse at any moment. Clinically, the only classic obsessional symptom which tends to emerge with comparable clarity at the outset is that of choice: the subject is unable to make some decision, and this swiftly reveals a whole history of procrastinations and doubts.

Freud had set doubt at the centre of obsessional neurosis, arguing that it expressed a fundamental oscillation between love and hate, a polarity that was later elaborated by Abraham across different clinical structures. As Freud put it, "Doubt is in reality a doubt of [the obsessional's] own love – which ought to be the most certain thing in his whole mind; and it becomes diffused over everything else, and is especially apt to become displaced on to what is most insignificant and small" (Freud,1909d, p. 241). This initial doubt would then become generalised to all aspects of the subject's experience. It was Helene Deutsch who formalised this as the obsessional question, "Do I love or hate?", echoed by the later Lacanian formula, "Am I alive or dead?" (Deutsch, 1930). Although this derives from Serge Leclaire rather than Lacan, it is a staple of Lacanian accounts of obsessional neurosis. If the question of existence is inassimilable to the signifier, the subject remains caught at the level of this structural impasse.

Where the hysteric's question revolves around the homologous inability of language to answer the enigma of sexual identity, the obsessional's concerns his existence itself. This structural dilemma is then given an oedipal gloss. Freud had argued that the obsessional's death wishes are not simply unbridled aggressivity, but attempts to resolve a problem, as in German courts, where "suits were usually brought to an end, before judgement had been given, by the death of the parties to the dispute. Thus, in every conflict which enters their lives, they are on the lookout for the death of someone who is of importance to them, usually of someone they love – such as one of the parents, or a rival, or one of the objects of love between which their inclinations are wavering" (Freud, 1909d, p. 236).

In Lacan's reformulation, as the slave waits for the death of the master, he works. But not only are the fruits of his work purloined, the recognition of his being in these fruits is simply that of his own "not being there". Where he "is" lies in the anticipated moment of the master's death, after which, he thinks, he will live: in waiting for this, he identifies with the master, as dead, and in the meantime, all he can do is work, deceiving the master of his good intentions. This reworking of the master-slave relation is quite different from the thesis of the signifier's inability to resolve the question of being, yet both converge on the question imputed to the obsessional "Am I alive or dead?".

***

The formula has had remarkable success, and provides an interpretative lens for so many of the phenomena of obsession: the apparent affective mortification of the subject, the election of an imaginary other to act in one's place, the imposition of signifiers at every place where gaps in between signifiers threaten to appear, the avoidance of risk, the prolonged inhibition regarding any action, and so on. Lacan's explanations here operate at two levels: first of all, the structural inability of the signifier to respond to the question of existence, and secondly, the installation of the subject in a time of waiting for the death of the master, usually equated here with the father. Once the latter is dead, the subject imagines he will be able to act. This is not an empirical death, but more of an imagined or, indeed, conceptual death, that Lacan ascribed a dialectical function to. Death here is situated as the point of resolution of the subject's predicament.

This question theory of neurosis – following Heidegger's equation of human existence with a question – was a part of Lacan's elaboration in the 1950s, yet its formulation for obsessional neurosis is not always helpful today. It has often resulted in an inhibition of further research, with each case reduced to this tidy formula, and with adjacent problems being mopped up with descriptive terms. The variety of clinical phenomena here are subsumed under the binary of jouissance and the signifier, with the latter trying and failing to absorb the former. The complexity of both Freud and Lacan's analysis of obsession tends to be lost in this attempt at distillation. The endless referencing here of the Rat Man's "horror at pleasure of his own" as he describes the famous torture echoes the iteration of the "alive or dead" formula.

We should note that the clinical visibility of these disjunctions may produce diagnostic error. Psychotic subjects may speak openly about an oscillation in their feelings here, as they feel transitioned from apparent vitality to a state of utter mortification. The very sense of being alive is touched on and the subject may describe himself as quite literally dead. This is indeed so frequent that it has elicited numerous commentaries, including Lacan's remarks in the context of his discussion of the Schreber case. Mortification in obsession is entirely different, and does not involve a libidinal catastrophe but rather a self-imposed schema of libidinal control and, in many cases, what seems to be impoverished affect. But this is not as obvious as it may seem.

Paul Schilder was interested in the motor aspects of obsession, which he believed had been eclipsed by the idea that it was hysteria that had the monopoly on bodily symptoms in neurosis (Schilder, 1940). He thought that the reaction against proximity – that is, things being brought together – evident in touching, pushing, and throwing, will pass to the proximity of ideas, which will then be disconnected via the mechanism of isolation. The motor impulse, for Schilder, is thus primary, and although we might not agree with his rather simplistic formulation of the relation between action and thought, the fact remains that whereas an obsessional subject may admit the most violent and sexual thoughts to consciousness in his obsessional ideas, these will be disguised in his compulsions. Similarly, if the obsessional thought is most often something that the subject tries to renounce, the compulsion, on the contrary, must be executed.

Now, how can this help us to elaborate the question of mortification in obsession? Glover's distinction between the agonies of introjection and projection is illuminating here. At one level, it seems as if the obsessional subject has no emotion, but this is because the affects are compressed so closely together (Glover, 1935). To avoid the "violent pendulum-swing" between introjective and projective processes brought on by the infant's acute fluctuations in affect, they are treated by rapid alternation and a reduction in the time interval between them. A meshwork of affect is thus produced with the aim of producing ever finer alternations, which, if scrutinised, is effectively a compounding of what Glover sees as introjection mechanisms (touch) and projection mechanisms (contamination). The famous obsessional displacement – or centrifugal alternation – of affects thus aims to lessen the anxiety of too powerful an introjection or projection by interweaving them, with the result of what looks like a stable relation to one's object.

An obsessional subject described the constant battle between what he called two internal voices, one chastising him and one consoling him. The tension between them was so acute that he sought, in his analysis, to attenuate them and to go beyond the "ambivalence" that he assumed to be their source. To an extent, this proved possible, and now, as he put it, the perpetual conflict had "flattened out". "But when you eliminate emotion", he added "you feel that you don't feel emotion". The physical palpitations that now assailed him were there to remind him of what he was feeling, of what was left of emotion from this process of "flattening out". They were a sign, he said, "of being alive".

To reduce the complexity of this process to a failed attempt to absorb jouissance in the signifier or to the question of being alive or dead may in some way be helpful, but it draws attention away from other structural issues. Take the question of doubt once again. In his 1953 lecture on "The real, the symbolic and the imaginary", Lacan noted that for Freud "the obsessional neurotic always lives in the register of what involves the elements of greatest uncertainty; how long one's life will last, who one's biological father is, and so on. There is no perceptual proof of any of that in human reality" (Lacan, 1953b, p. 55). They are all built up out of symbolic elements, and hence "the question of doubt is much closer to the symbolic constitution of reality. It is in some sense preliminary to it" (ibid.). The obsessional's question then concerns the symbolic itself, yet his doubt is secondary to a basic act of faith, the *Urglaube* that Husserl saw as the condition of symbolic registration.

The logic here follows the same sequence sketched out by Freud and later by Jones (1918) and Karin Stephen (1933): what generates the impasse for the obsessional is then used to treat it. If language is the source of uncertainty, it is language that supplies the apparent remedy, in an obviously circular process. We could note that this perspective is not compatible with Freud's theorisation of uncertainty: the focus on the structural feature of language is different from that on the unresolved tension between love and hate which Freud saw as the motor of doubt. It is this same circularity that Lacan will elaborate with great subtlety in his distinction between the demand for death and the death of demand in *Formations of the Unconscious* (Lacan, 1957–1958).

***

Lacan's commentary here shifts the earlier emphasis from the relations to the paternal figure to the phallus and the question of the early dependency on the mother. The obsessional perceives very well the place of the phallus in the mother's desire, and chooses to destroy it while at the same time preserving it in order to sustain his own desire. It is because desire – and demand – are first and foremost articulated in the Other that the conditions of his impasse are created. If he tries to express desire here, it is extinguished, and hence it can only be approached via a denial. Because of the priority of the Other as the place of the signifier, this denial is the only way that desire can be approached.

This gives the rhythm of cruelty and solicitude so manifest in the obsessional's object relations, and his despair at damage to his possessions. And yet we could note here how losses often seem remarkably painless for the obsessional – presumably due to the equivalence of his sexual objects – while the breaking of a vase or the tearing of a piece of clothing can generate utter despair. To evoke a bodily investment here only partly explains this asymmetry, as the sexual object is usually chosen precisely in order to supply this same investment at the point where the ego experiences its most critical point of weakness.

The question of death and the destruction of the phallus is elaborated by Lacan in *Formations of the Unconscious* (1957–1958) and then in the *Transference* seminar (1960–1961). Striking it is left as an unrealised possibility, left at times to the Others whom the obsessional chooses as his more virile friends or idols. Lacan nuances his thesis here to claim that the obsessional doesn't aim exactly at a destruction of the desire of the Other but at "a rejection of its signs". This is accompanied by a close reading of Maurice Bouvet's 1949 case of Renée, taken as an exemplar of obsession (Bouvet, 1950). The problem here is that no one today could seriously agree with this diagnosis, a fact which perhaps explains why Lacanian commentaries on the case are so scarce.

This puzzled me for a long time until I realised that the dynamics that Lacan describes so finely perhaps apply not to Bouvet's patient but to Lacan's relation to Bouvet himself. There can't have been such a sustained campaign against one analyst by another in the whole history of psychoanalysis, and Lacan's animosity towards Bouvet dwarfs the Freud-Jung conflict, saturating Lacan's writings and seminars for almost a decade in both explicit and implicit form. The attacks are just so relentless that it is difficult not to infer that the preservation of Bouvet as his rival may have had a certain function for Lacan.

We should add to this problematic of the phallus a feature present in Lacan's commentary on the Rat Man and which we find in so many cases of obsessional neurosis. In "The neurotic's individual myth", Lacan uses Lévi-Strauss's algebraic formula for myth as a template to approach the dynamics of the case (Lacan, 1953a). Although he does not make this explicit in the text, his reliance on the formula is obvious, and I have discussed it in detail elsewhere (Leader, 1993). This use of a formula is interesting in itself, as the appeal to algebra would occur explicitly a few years later in the seminar on object relations (Lacan, 1956–1957), where the same formula is used to order the case material of Little Hans and to formalise the mythic constructions that mark the end of the boy's phobia. Curiously, despite Lacan's efforts, there seems to be not a single case in the whole of Lacanian literature where this algebraic approach has been adopted. This is even more curious given the fact that Lacan's conclusions regarding both the Rat Man and Hans are routinely cited with approval.

This is a pity, and especially so since combinatorial problems lie at the heart of obsession. Lévi-Strauss had introduced the algebra of the transformation group in 1945, and developed it a few years later in his *Elementary Structures of Kinship* (1949a) where marriage and descent are seen as structures that can be combined and inverted. By 1957 Lacan is using his own formulation of the transformation group, where an equation is identified with a group of permutations, representing the symmetry properties of the equation. Now, what would such properties consist of? For Lacan, as for Lévi-Strauss, they involve running through different forms of an impossibility. As Lévi-Strauss puts it, "The inability to connect two (contradictory) relationships is overcome/replaced by the positive statement that contradictory relationships are identical inasmuch as they are both self-contradictory in a similar way" (Lévi-Strauss, 1955, p. 216). This is formalised as $Fx(a) : Fy (b) = Fx(b) : Fa -1 (y)$.

In other words, an equivalence relation is established between two situations which are self-contradictory in a similar way, such that there is an inversion of terms and relations. One term is replaced by its contrary and an inversion is made between the function and the term value of two elements. Lacan singles out two elements here from the family constellation of the Rat Man:

1. The father married a woman of higher station, privileging a rich girl over a poor one.
2. The father contracted a gambling debt, from which he was saved by a friend whom he then failed to repay.

The complexities of the Rat Man's obsessive activities around reimbursement following the loss of his glasses are then formulated as ciphering the contradictory relation between 1. and 2., which involve debts that cannot be superimposed the one on the other. Without going into the details of the transformations here, the Rat Man aims to superimpose

3. His giving money to Lieutenant A, repaying a debt to a friend.

Onto:

4. Lieutenant A giving money to the lady at the post office, repaying a debt.

The debt is paid back to a woman who, at the same time, is not repaid, as she has in fact given the money to Lieutenant B, which means that she ends up with nothing. So, the contradiction "to repay a woman: a woman is not repaid" ciphers the double debt of the father with a new form of contradiction. The relation is "parallel" in the sense that it concerns a debt, and "inverted" in that it pays the rich girl and not the friend (Leader, 1993).

The question of the gambling debt is knotted to that of the father's object choice, which embodies a fault both in terms of a betrayal of love (the rich girl over the poor one) and in the social and economic imbalance of the marriage. Case after case shows us how fault lines in kinship relations are worked and reworked by the subject, generating an ever-expanding set of impossibilities. The complexity of the logical structures here is avoided with formulas such as "desire for the obsessional is impossible", and the fault lines themselves are often reduced to appeals to the "jouissance of the Other", with the Rat Man's expression of horror mixed with pleasure elevated to iconic status. Yet these fault lines are more complex, and Lacan's insistence on their place at a symbolic level can be verified clinically.

What form can such fault lines take? An act of marriage between members of the same family, an expectation of marital or romantic symmetry between the children of different families, second or third marriages that complicate lineages and, more generally, any fault lines in the family constellation revolving around the exchange of women. To reduce these to instances of the "jouissance of the Other" is to miss the point slightly, as the reason why the neurosis generates around such points is not reducible to a treatment of jouissance but to a much broader question about kinship structures.

Indeed, in Lacan's discussion of the Rat Man, he is less interested in the encounter with the cruel captain's enjoyment than in the network of exchanges and failed exchanges that precede the subject's birth. Lacan follows Lévis-Strauss here, who had argued, in a text that Lacan knew well, that it is less the traumatic encounter that matters than the "crystallisation" it produces in the subject, which will be "molded by a pre-existing structure" (Lévi-Strauss, 1949b, p. 202). Or, to put it another way, the neurosis is not just a question of trauma but of trauma plus algebra.

We could add here that it is unlikely that the particularity of the father's gambling debt was lost on his son. He had used the regimental funds, which he had been entrusted with safeguarding. If the friend had not come to his rescue, we might wonder what a military man might have done faced with this utter disgrace. In this sense, the construction around the loss of his glasses is built up around the imagined point of the father's self-inflicted death: a compulsive repayment to bolster the loan supplied by the friend, at the horizon of which is death.

What we see in obsession is the subject struggling to situate symbolically these fault lines. If in phobia the subject generates a series of situations that play out an initial impossibility in different forms – the permutations of Little Hans – in obsession a combinatorial problem leaves its mark on the subject's sexual life. Hence it is perhaps no accident that Lacan uses exactly the same Lévi-Strauss algebra for both Hans and the Rat Man. The impossibility with which Lacan characterised obsessional desire is not simply a function of the denial of the desire of the Other, but may result from the combinatorial dilemma of a problematic exchange of women which, from the subject's perspective, is impossible.

***

Lacan's combinatorial approach resituates the Freudian problem of love and hate, just as it offers a new understanding of the way in which symptoms include pairs of opposites which are apparently inconsistent. If an oscillation between love and hate is central in obsessional neurosis, to the extent that Deutsch would cast it as the defining question "Do I love or hate?", it now becomes an effect of a symbolic process of generating self-contradictory – or conflictual – propositions. The affective polarities are the result of a structural fault line which seeks out and generates further polarities to perpetuate its algebraic stasis. We can remember here that this process did not constitute a solution, in Lévi-Strauss terms, but a reposing of a problem. Although we are not obliged to accept this reformulation, it is clear that obsessional neurosis cannot be reduced to any kind of quantitative issue of love and hate, along the lines of: "The future obsessional's hate is greater than his love."

This may also help us to clarify the function of guilt in obsession. It is well-known that although the obsessional subject may complain of feeling guilty, he loves his guilt as himself. Freud saw this as an archaic positioning in relation to sexual experience: the subject marks the trauma with guilt, in relation to the excess of pleasure that he felt.

Yet, as he would later argue, there is more than one kind of guilt. If there is a guilt linked to what the subject has done or felt or thought, there is also a more structural guilt, transmitted intergenerationally, that Freud explored in *Totem and Taboo* (1912–1913). The murder of the father by the band of brothers creates a guilt that is situated at the origin of social organisation, and transmitted through each subsequent phase of history. This is clearly not the same as the guilt that a subject may feel when he enjoys some form of sexual arousal "too much".

Lacan elaborated exactly this distinction between a guilt associated with acts and a structural guilt linked to one's filiations in the symbolic. Where Martin Buber had elaborated his own version of this polarity in 1957, distinguishing a guilt linked to childhood arousal and a guilt linked to perturbations to "the order" of things, Lacan first of all separates a guilt produced by this very "order" and then distinguishes this latter guilt from what he saw as a more modern problem (Buber, 1957). Using the concept of Ate, understood as the signifying transmission between generations, linked to destiny and kinship structures, "the debt that constitutes our fate", a first guilt is equated with its basic inscription. We are guilty of the "charge" we receive from this symbolic that precedes us.

Distinguishing a guilt linked to the violation of taboos and this more fundamental "ontic" guilt was already articulated in Buber, but Lacan goes further here. A third guilt is now defined less as the effect of a symbolic debt than as a forced separation from the debt itself. In the *Transference* seminar (1960–1961), Lacan evokes those cases where the debt that determines one's place is in effect stolen. With the contemporary devaluation of the very concept of Ate and its "implacable order of debt", the idea of fate no longer has any resonance and the symbolic inscription in a lineage of debt is undermined. Giving up one's Ate, "as we can now", Lacan argues, makes us even more responsible than before. Our modern guilt, he concludes, is the guilt that the God of fate is dead (ibid., p. 358).

This distinction between two kinds of guilt is salient to obsessional neurosis, and it should draw our attention both to the structural function of guilt and to the impasse of confusing them. Although the subject can always find new things to feel guilty about, a more fundamental guilt is intergenerationally bound and is, in fact, absolutely necessary for him. If a problem in the exchange of women has marked his family history, involving the lack of respect of a symbolic boundary, guilt is there to re-establish a boundary. Of course, it doesn't do this job very well, and even less so given the confusions between the two distinct registers of guilt. Focusing on an empirical guilt linked to some trespass will have little effect on the more structural guilt that has this crucial function of standing in for the law of prohibition. Guilt here takes the place of an interdiction that could not be properly inscribed: the subject uses guilt to – unsuccessfully – create a prohibition at the point of the symbolic fault.

Lacan's emphasis on what he called the "pact of speech" involves precisely this dimension of a fault in the symbolic constellation of the subject. Advising against any attempt to "reintegrate the subject into his ego", he encouraged the exploration of the subject's family history to pinpoint the "broken stitches" that preceded his arrival in the world. This echoes the consequences of distinguishing between different registers of guilt: it will only make things worse to try to persuade the subject that he shouldn't feel guilty. Rather, it is a question of separating the empirical guilts and the structural guilt linked to these symbolic fault lines, and of recognising its function. Needless to say, a direct communication of this to the patient is useless.

This also sheds light on the obsessional's well-known tendency to seek authorisation for any new romantic interest. If love life is linked to the non-respect of a symbolic principle of regulation, any new encounter will call for some third party to sanction it. The problem here is that as well as appealing to his Others, the obsessional has his own issues of control. As Jones showed, taking up Freud's term, there is always a powerful *Eigensinn* here, a self-willedness, or obstinacy, to give a chronic attitude of defiance. Unlike the more visible refusals of the hysteric, the obsessional may well say Yes but harbour a No, resenting all forms of external influence and interference.

Lacan redrafts these dynamics in terms of demand and desire, and being and having. Rather than the competition of desire and demand so prevalent in hysteria, the obsessional tries to produce a coalescence of the two, suspending himself from the demand of the Other, and aiming to substitute demand for desire itself. We could note that this might involve in one case an aspiration and in another an avoidance. At the level of castration, the subject takes refuge in not-having, a strategy designed to allow him to harbour his being in peace, thus sidestepping the price of his membership of the symbolic. We can see this in many phenomena, from action by proxy in love life to the false humility so common in the world of academe.

This should alert us to another common misconception about obsessional neurosis. We often hear it said that the obsessional seeks a consistent Other, and mobilises compulsions at any point of inconsistency to ward off the signs of the desire of the Other. This is of course often the case, but what we see beyond it is the obsessional's very particular choice of Other: precisely an inconsistent one. The Rat Man would choose Freud as his analyst with the idea that he concealed some quite unsavoury qualities, and beyond immediate idealisations this is an Other that is imagined to hide some guilty secret. Why the inconsistency? The strategy here is simple: so that the subject can lodge his own fault in the point of inconsistency in the Other. He hides his desire where he thinks that the Other is himself hiding something.

The early analysts had been alert to the duplicity of the transference here, linking this effort to preserve being to toilet training. For Jones, the subject aims to retain control of the act of shitting principally via postponement, yet the regulation of sphincters is first and foremost in the service of others. He controls himself for the sake of someone else, to generate an often subtle choreography of demand. In toilet training, after all, the subject must do not what he wishes but what he is told. He works for the Other here, but smuggles in his own non-compliance via postponement, in the same way that the office worker can say "yes" to the tasks imposed on him yet sabotage any result by completing them too late or imperfectly. As Karin Stephen pointed out, there is a difference here between acquiescence and consent (Stephen, 1933, p. 142). The obsessional may submit to toilet training and do what he is asked to do, yet this does not mean that he has consented to it. On the contrary, he obeys through fear, a distinction that is evident in many areas of the obsessional's customs and habits.

This is evident not only in the position that many subjects take in relation to their work and professional organisation, but also in relation to theory itself. Think, for example, of the popularity of the version of Lacanianism that emphasises the imposition of language on the organism, leaving a remainder in the form of object a. Repeated again and again, with no focus on or interest in the particularity of such a process, it is difficult not to see it as another form of the obsessional's toilet-based vision of the world: one thing is substituted for another, leaving an unsymbolisable remainder. Religion here shares with psychoanalysis a fascination with the left-over, even if the treatments given to this are very different.

The question of how psychoanalysis engages with the obsessional here is of course linked to that of how the obsessional engages with psychoanalysis. Ferenczi observed long ago that as a practice, analysis seems ideally suited to sustain and nourish the defensive system of the obsessional. What could be better than free association, after all, for avoiding certain topics? The obsessional would only be following a rule in saying what he likes, and hence the necessity for the analyst to intervene, at times, against association. If hysterics invented psychoanalysis, it is obsessionals who are responsible for all its technical innovations, from Ferenczi's "active technique" to Lacan's "variable sessions". Obsession here, in its resistance to analysis and in its tendency towards inertia, can – at least in principle – push analysis towards something new.

References

Bouvet, M. (1950). Incidences therapeutiques de la prise de conscience de l'envie du penis dans la nevrose obsessionelle feminine. *Revue Française de Psychanalyse, 19*: 215–243.

Buber, M. (1957). Guilt and guilt feelings. *Psychiatry, 20 (2)*: 114–129.

Deutsch, H. (1930). Obsessional Ideas. In: H. Deutsch, *Neuroses and Character Types*: 134–144. New York: International Universities Press, 1965.

Freud, S. (1909d). Notes upon a case of obsessional neurosis. *S. E., 10*: 151–318. London: Hogarth, 1955.

Freud, S. (1912–1913). *Totem and Taboo. S. E., 13*: vii-162. London: Hogarth, 1953.

Glover, E. (1935). A developmental study of the obsessional neuroses. *International Journal of Psychoanalysis, 16*: 131–144.

Jones, E. (1918). Hate and anal erotism in the obsessional neurosis. In: E. Jones, *Papers on Psycho-Analysis, 2nd ed.* London: Ballière, Tindall and Cox, pp. 540–548.

Lacan, J. (1953a). The neurotic's individual myth. M. N. Evans (Trans.). *Psychoanalytic Quarterly, 1979, 48*: 405–425.

Lacan, J. (1953b). Le symbolique, l'imaginaire et le reel. In: J. Lacan, *Des Noms-du-Pere*. Paris: Seuil, 2005, pp. 11–63

Lacan, J. (1956–1957). *Le Séminaire, Livre IV, La relation d'objet*. J.-A. Miller (Ed.). Paris: Seuil,1994.

Lacan, J. (1957–1958). *The Seminar of Jacques Lacan, Book V, Formations of the Unconscious*. J.-A. Miller (Ed.), R. Grigg (Trans.). Cambridge: Polity, 2017.

Lacan, J. (1960–1961). *The Seminar of Jacques Lacan, Book VIII, Transference*. J.-A. Miller (Ed.), B. Fink (Trans.). Cambridge: Polity, 2015.

Lévi-Strauss, C. (1949a). *Elementary Structures of Kinship*. R. Needham (Ed.), J. H. Bell and J. R. V. Sturmer (Trans.). Boston: Beacon, 1969.

Lévi-Strauss, C. (1949b). The Effectiveness of Symbols. In: C. Lévi-Strauss, *Structural Anthropology*: 186–205. New York: Basic Books, 1963.

Lévi-Strauss, C. (1955). The Structural Study of Myth. In: C. Lévi-Strauss, *Structural Anthropology*: 206–231. New York: Basic Books, 1963.

Leader, D. (1993). Some notes on obsessional neurosis. *Journal of the Centre for Freudian Analysis and Research, 2*: 34–43.

Rado, S. (1959). Obsessive Behaviour. In: S. Arieti (Ed.). *American Handbook of Psychiatry, Vol 1*: 34–344. New York: Basic Books.

Schilder, P. (1940). The structure of obsessions and compulsions. *Psychiatry, 3*: 549–60.

Stephen, K. (1933). *The Wish to Fall Ill*. Cambridge: Cambridge University Press, 1960.

CHAPTER THREE

The signification of debt in obsessional neurosis[1]

MOUSTAPHA SAFOUAN

When Freud's patient known by the strange epithet the "Rat Man" was born in 1878, how was he welcomed by his father – in other words, by the man who was to recognise him as his son in the eyes of the Lord? It was with the following words: "He thought that they would have to cut down expenses after all, as there would be an extra person living in the house now."[2] "So many children, so many *kronen*", we might be tempted to add. Or perhaps, in terms slightly different from those used by the patient, let us say that for this father, who owed his fortune to his wife's family, each new-born child signified the renewed demand of his own waste products – the only objects that the human being "produces himself". Here I am referring to Freud, who commented on this pronouncement as follows: "Something else lay behind this, *viz* that his father liked having his permission asked, as though he wanted to abuse his power, although perhaps he was really only enjoying the feeling that everything came from him."[3] Everything – including the new arrivals!

The son strikes back at the father in a dream[4] in which the former takes ownership of the father's enunciation of despair (to the extent of thinking it rather than saying it out loud), while the latter plays the role of the one who returns after a long absence. His return, by the way, does not

51

surprise the dreamer in the least. His father arrives at the appointed hour, like a monthly allowance; and we all know that it is stools that are the first thing demanded from a child, at the right moment and not at any other.[5]

So, we can see how the father's fault recurs in the son: the unpaid debt of the former – to recognise his son as anything other than a waste product – will shackle the latter in return.

In truth, in both cases the fault is related to the act – that which I have done which I ought not to have done, and that which I have not done which I ought to have done. In every case, it entails a sanction for which I am liable until justice is finally done. In this case, it is not a real fault; the Rat Man was not the result of the most accursed of all unions. If Oedipus sinned in that way, he did so unwittingly, and that should have sufficed to excuse him. But doubtless this aspect of the myth has the value of pointing something out to us: that the fault in question is situated beyond everything the subject can say about it; it belongs in the realm of origins, which is lost to us, in that place where the subject would have no means of enunciating it, however great his efforts, however complex the scaffolding he tries to erect in order to attach his fault to one or another of his acts, except in terms of "the human condition". And so, we are now going to try to articulate the relation of fault to not-knowing, or to the not-known of the subject.

***

In order to do this, let us look at Freud's paper "Two principles of mental functioning" (Freud, 1911b), in which he develops an apparently very simple argument. Two opposing principles govern psychical life: the reality principle and the pleasure principle. A psychical process falls within the domain of either the one or the other of these principles. Repression, which consists in a turning away from pain, or from everything that produces an increase in the level of tension, clearly falls under the sway of the pleasure principle. As a result, one might expect this process to be directed towards reality, and for it to overcome any disappointment, humiliation or offence we might have been exposed to in this reality. However, this is not the case. By the time he wrote this paper (1911b), Freud had long since abandoned his trauma theory. According to him, repression overcomes our desires and our fantasies; in other words, precisely those things without which there is neither pleasure nor even any quest for pleasure.

In my view, the "revolutionary" impact of the Freudian discovery of the Oedipus scenario resides not in a renewal of the myth, but rather in the fact that it allowed the formulation of this paradox, which, while it may escape the notice of the cursory reader, certainly did not escape the attention of its author.

Indeed, Freud tried at the very least to explain the direction taken by repression, pointing out that it is characteristic of our unconscious wishes to be assimilated into realities – a feature with which no analyst "can become accustomed without the exercise of great self-discipline" (Freud, 1911b, p. 225). For example, I have murderous wishes towards my father; the longed-for murder is considered to have been committed already, and is treated as such: I turn away from it, and want to know nothing of its existence, or the part that I played in it.

What does this mean? Since the unconscious desire *existed*, but only until the moment when the repression was lifted, that is to say, until the moment when there was a passage to knowledge, we have to conclude that the murder, or the murderous desire, was hiding in the not-knowing, that it *existed* all the while I didn't *know* anything about it, and that was the sole condition for its existence. There is an incompatibility in principle between the knowledge and the truth of desire[6]. I want to know, I consent to know, as much as you wish, provided that nothing of the truth of this desire itself becomes caught up in the knowing: it is on this condition that the existence of oedipal desire is based. Fundamentally, the reality principle is not in opposition to the pleasure principle, since it "safeguards" it, as Freud put it. It is truth itself which is "a stranger to reality (cf., Lacan, "The Freudian Thing", in: Lacan, 1966, pp. 334–363). On this subject, the example that Freud gives us towards the end of his paper is worthy of our attention in a number of ways.

He tells of a patient who dreams of his father, who has recently died: the father speaks to him just as he did when he was alive; but the patient has the painful realisation that his father is dead, but he does not know it. And Freud notes that this nonsensical dream makes sense if the text is completed thus: he doesn't know that he was dead according to the patient's wish.

"He was dead but he didn't know it." And for sure, there was no way of disabusing him: "Father, you are dead!" without evoking an echo of the guilty wish. Guilt arises each time I approach the repressed, and it blocks the path along which I might reach it; it works in the same direction as repression, which itself is not motivated by guilt; on the contrary, there is guilt because there is repression.

Let us suppose in any case that I communicate this knowledge I have at my disposal to the father. What would happen then? He would return to nothingness.

But if there is some necessity to allow him to believe in this semblance of existence, is this "allowing to believe" not all the more necessary in order that I can believe the same thing of myself? Because, in the end, it is in the rival, the imago in which the fragmentation and the rupture of castration appear to have been overcome, that death and castration are first misrecognised. It is a misrecognition in which, initially, prehistorically, I recognise myself.

There is something similar going on in rivalry and in the "He did not know" uselessly attributed to this other who is called my father; but from now on, can there be any relation to the real, other than that to which that name commits me?

***

To what extent do these considerations assist us in illuminating the signification of debt in obsessional neurosis? The answer to that can come only from applying them to a particular example, once again borrowed from the Rat Man case.

We know that when Captain Novak had asked him to repay the sum of 3.80 *kronen* to Lieutenant A, the Rat Man reacted as if it was a question of an imperative imposed by the will of the captain, which he had to carry out to the letter, even though he knew that the captain had made a mistake regarding the identity of the creditor. The Rat Man initially responded to this "order" unconsciously, in ways that Freud miraculously reconstituted for us: "As sure as my father and the lady can have children, I'll pay him back the money!" (Freud, 1909d, p. 218). A response which, as we can see, implies a reference to what we, following Freud, can call the "superior knowledge" in the Other, who clearly was not Captain N, who obviously had no knowledge at all of the intimate life of the subject.

The fact that the response was unconscious signifies that the subject did not in the least want to set foot in any place whatsoever where he could come across this knowledge. And yet, he knew! He knew his father could not have children, since he had already been dead for several years.

Similarly, he knew (and it is he who let us know this) that the lady had had both ovaries removed. Certainly. But that is not the question; the question is: "What about the Other – does he know?" Because the fact that the Other is the locus of a certain knowledge does not mean that he knows; quite the contrary. Let us scrutinise this more closely.

It would be easy to demonstrate that all the Rat Man's surges of appetite were aimed towards re-finding his sister Katherine, who, how-ever, was dead. It was her unforgettable pronouncement: "On my soul, if you die I shall kill myself" (ibid., p. 264), which was, definitively, the reason why he chose life over death. Was it a case of a refusal to mourn? There are some ambiguities here. For we could also say that since her death, the Rat Man had been living in an interminable state of mourn-ing. We know of his predilection for funerals and condolences, which had earned him the nickname "carrion crow". Taken as a whole, his position was one of despair, but mercifully this was hidden from him: no oracle had revealed it to him, as the three witches had to Macbeth, promising him everything (though he had to work for it, and in a crimi-nal way), except what was his due, namely his desire for offspring. The Rat Man could not bring his mourning to an end, because he could not allow it to increase, if we can put it that way, or to begin the "work" of mourning, according to Freud's implacable expression. And how could he, without giving up his raison d'être, apply himself to the task of fac-ing the knowledge a second time that his sister was irretrievably lost? Unless some form of mediation had signified to him that bringing back Katherine was in nobody's gift, not even that of his father, or indeed of any father; so that facing this limitation of the power of the father he could have accepted the same limitation for himself, and even been able to console himself by becoming a father in turn.[7]

And yet did he not know of this impossibility, just as we do? For sure he did. But has the knowledge we have, or think we have, prevented us from treating children as if they were revenants, and speaking of them as if they could replace one another, or de-throne one another; in short, as if the only thing that really counted for us were the place that they successively occupy, which is always occupied even though it is actually empty? It takes the genius of a Veronese ("Moses saved from the water", in the Prado) to give us an idea of how flabbergasted one would be to see a child for the first time who has no familiar features whatsoever. It is thus not sufficient to know a thing in order not to for-get it. If that were the case, there would be no "return of the repressed".

Similarly, the Rat Man knew just as well as the lady what sort of surgery she had had. But did she know? Or, more precisely, how efficacious was this knowledge for her? Probably not at all. There is nothing to stop us imagining that the lady would have wished to have children, and all the more ardently since she knew she was unable to have them. What a catharsis both of pity and of fear would have been involved in saying this to her! Moreover, to say it to her without having received the message from her, in other words, outside the context of analysis, would have been nothing but an affront. When Freud writes that his patient, who loved children very much, hesitated to marry the lady because he knew it would be impossible to fulfil his desire with her, we have to observe that this was absolutely not the case. In the *Rat Man* case there is no indication whatsoever of any wavering in his desire to marry the lady, any more than there was any wavering between the lady, for whom his love was "indestructible", and another woman; in his eyes there was no other worthy of being her rival. We will not expatiate here on the Rat Man's infatuation, which, clinically speaking, was somewhat disturbing. But we can get the measure of it, not from his lack of comprehension of death – for his was no greater or lesser than our own – but from his incapacity to grasp that death itself sets the limit to his own comprehension; in other words, as Freud put it, to notice the flaw in reasoning inherent in his cogitations on the subject. All the same, it was clearly because of his knowledge regarding the barrenness of the lady that in fantasy he flooded her with his semen – her, Gisela (we know that her first name was included unwittingly in the very enunciation of his fantasy, composed of the first letters of his prayers), and that he clung to it exclusively and unconditionally. In a word, when he thought unconsciously, "As sure as my father and the lady can have children", the Rat Man was enunciating, or rather keeping quiet, the very impossibility on which his desire was founded.

He signified this problematic with the greatest eloquence in his dream of the two Japanese swords, in which he proposed liberating the lady with the two swords, which in the dream signified "marriage" and "copulation". But then just as he was preparing to do so, he became confused, no longer knowing whether he was liberating her with the two swords, or keeping her prisoner.[8]

"Marriage": that is to say the word closest to its function of union, in so far as the subject assumes a choice in it, but also in its extreme vanity, since it is an oath. Let us say it plainly: social and religious morality cannot alter the fact that when a lover swears fidelity, or demands that someone swears fidelity to him, we can be quite sure, as analysts, that he is frantically trying to compete with the phallus. But to the very extent that phallicism dominates his choice of object – and the profoundly reparative nature of the Rat Man's desire shows rather well that this was certainly true in his case – it is the "sword of copulation" that does not follow suit. The alternative in the dream signifies that it is impossible to be the phallus and to have it at the same time.

So, it is clear that the Rat Man was mistaken when he promised himself children from his marriage to the lady, and that the phallus (as, no doubt, the removal of the ovaries for her[9]), was from then on nothing other than the support of the fantasy which was maintained – oh! jouissance – by its fundamental rebellion against any "reality testing". The alternative in the dream signifies in another dimension: it is impossible to use words to deceive oneself and to disabuse oneself at the same time, in the same way that it is impossible both to make use of one's phallus and to retain it as the simulacrum of a jouissance which is both enigmatic and closed-off.[10]

But attempting the impossible is precisely what the obsessional does. When Captain N asked him to pay A, the Rat Man's first reaction was to say to himself: "You are not to pay back the money, or the fantasy about the rats will come true as regards the people you love the most [his father and the lady]." In that case, as Freud demonstrated, it was not a question of refusal, but of veritable derision. Also, he was eager to carry out Captain N's "order" to the letter, forgetting, through a secondary and symptomatic repression, what he knew from another source: that Captain N was making a mistake, since it was not Lieutenant A but the female post-office employee who had paid for the pince-nez ordered from Vienna. Thus, his impotent desire ended up trumping his "better knowledge": "Let them have children all the same!"

Such was the *fiat* which Captain Novak's story constituted – which emerged, to the detriment of the Rat Man, at a sort of fertile moment when he was wavering between two conquests, a waitress in an inn and the woman who worked in the post office – and it meant that he caught a glimpse of the horrifying image. In spite of the desperate attempt at exorcism it entailed, the false debt with which the Rat Man burdened himself was nothing other than the ceremonial in which he sustained his jouissance, beyond what he failed at.

The more the subject creates an obligation to an *imaginary* debt, the more he becomes shackled by the *symbolic* debt, which is transmitted along with the fault. And anyone who wants to absolve the patient of it without himself becoming embroiled, needs first of all to know how to tell these two apart. *Scilicet.*

Notes

1. Title of the seminar for the year 1968–1969.
2. See the French translation of Freud's observations in *Lettres de l'École freudienne de Paris*, No. 5, p. 38 (Freud, 1907–1908) and *Standard Edition* Vol. X, p. 298, where we read that the father "was in despair over his birth, as he was over each new baby" (Freud, 1909d).
3. *Loc. cit.*, p. 38; *S. E.*, 10, p. 298; our italics.
4. *Loc. cit.*, p. 38; *S. E.*, p. 298.
5. A patient of ours commented on his mother's rigidity in this matter, in a discourse (constituted, among other things, by a certain elaborate ratiocination involving the letter *A*, which occurred repeatedly in "caca" as well as "papa") which revealed a rather uncharitable thought which, after a certain amount of working through, could be expressed thus: "Just look at the monogram she has chosen for the organ!" Neurosis is a misrecognition of the fact that "creation begins with the letter *B*", we might say; and the primal scene is traumatic only in so far as the subject is close to deciphering, if we may put it that way, this very misrecognition.
6. And not between truth and the law, as some simpletons never stop repeating.
7. In this knowledge resides the "second death" evoked by Lacan in his memorable seminar *The Ethics of Psychoanalysis* (1959–1960). It is because this "knowing how to read" is closed off that those we call psychotic have no recourse other than to realise this "second death" in real death.
8. *Loc. cit.* p. 8, *S. E.*, 10, p. 267.
9. The Rat Man himself drew a parallel between the lady's operation and the fact that one of his testicles remained undescended; this happened in a dream which showed, in the clearest possible way, that it was only to the extent that he made his penis into an insignia of virility (in the same way as the three stars are the military sign of the captain) that the subject felt himself inadequate, even though his sexual potency was otherwise normal.

10. The analysis of many dreams has taught us that the alternative in the manifest content of the dream indicates the presence of an alternative in the latent content. We know that according to Freud, the alternative indicates the failure of the dream to unify two ideas. This thesis is difficult to accept, since Freud does not tell us the reasons for this failure, while the dream constantly succeeds in achieving such unification elsewhere. Moreover, our interpretation could easily be applied to Freud's principal example: his dream the night following the death of his father. And the signification of that would be as follows: it is useless to expect to be forgiven (the closing of an eye) by one who is not supposed to know of the fault (closing both eyes).

References

Freud, S. (1907–1908). L'Homme aux Rats. Notes originales du cas. *Lettres de l'École freudienne de Paris, 5,* 1968.

Freud, S. (1909d). Notes upon a case of obsessional neurosis. *S. E., 10:* 151–318. London: Hogarth, 1955.

Freud, S. (1911b). Formulations on the two principles of mental functioning, *S. E., 12:* 213–226. London: Hogarth, 1958.

Lacan, J. (1959–1960). *The Seminar of Jacques Lacan, Book VII, The Ethics of Psychoanalysis.* J.-A. Miller (Ed.), D. Porter (Trans.). New York: Norton, 1992.

Lacan, J. (1966). *Écrits.* B. Fink (Trans.). New Work: Norton, 2002.

CHAPTER FOUR

The cutting edge of desire in obsessional neurosis
Lacan with Leclaire

LUCA BOSETTI

In the twenty-second lecture of *Seminar V, Formations of the Unconscious* (Lacan,1957–1958), Lacan draws attention to a problem concerning obsessional neurosis. Psychoanalysts, according to Lacan, can have a hard time when it comes to discerning and articulating appropriately the fundamental components of obsessional neurosis. Lacan illustrates this difficulty by referring to Plato's famous metaphor of the "clumsy butcher" or "clumsy cook" in the *Phaedrus* (Plato, 1952, p. 133). In Plato's dialogue the clumsy butcher represents the philosopher who is not capable of dividing up his subject of enquiry "according to its parts" and following its "natural" or "objective" articulations, just like a bad butcher who would hack off and splinter body parts in a clumsy way. Likewise, for Lacan, psychoanalysts may become confused by the extremely varied clinical manifestations of obsessional neurosis and fail to articulate it appropriately at its structural joints, both in their practice and in their theoretical work.

In the remaining sessions of *Seminar V* Lacan tries to show a possible way out of this difficulty. Like a "good cook" who "knows how to cut at the joints" he tries to develop a theory of obsessional neurosis starting not from "the diversity of aspects it presents" but from its distinctive structural joints (Lacan, 1957–1958, p. 377). The "carving tool" he utilises to dismember appropriately obsessional neurosis is the concept of desire, which he introduces and elaborates carefully in the first part of the seminar. Lacan defines neurosis as a *relationship* to desire, as a particular way that the subject can find to "consist as a subject" in relation to desire (ibid., p. 377). The paradigmatic modality of the subject's relationship to desire is what is used by Lacan to identify the basic joint, the primary cutting off point or differentiation from which it is possible to then articulate the other distinctive characteristics of the obsessional structure.

Interestingly, the butchery metaphor with which Lacan opens his discussion of obsessional neurosis in *Seminar V* is echoed in a few remarks with which, a few months after the end of his seminar, Lacan commented on a case presented by Serge Leclaire at a meeting of the *Evolution Psychiatrique* group in Paris. Lacan's comments are transcribed and can be read at the end of the text of Leclaire's presentation, titled "The obsessional and his desire" and published in the group's journal one year later (Lacan, 1959). Lacan starts by praising Leclaire's way of constructing the case, and particularly Leclaire's ability to start from the "particularities" of the case to access the "universal signification of desire" (ibid., p. 409f). He then highlights Leclaire's ability to make evident in this way – from its "particularities" and from the "signification of desire" – the structural joints of the case, and contrasts it with the way most analysts fail to adequately "segment" and "dismember" obsessional neurosis, thus pointing to Leclaire as an exemplary "good butcher" of obsessional neurosis (ibid., p. 409).

A relationship to desire

Lacan starts his dismembering of obsessional neurosis in *Seminar V* from the idea that what defines obsessional neurosis is a relationship [*rapport*] to desire (Lacan, 1957–1958, p. 442). In this part of the seminar Lacan uses the idea of "relationship to desire" in two main ways.

On the one hand, "relationship to desire" refers to the subject's confrontation with desire as a point of articulation or "joint" that has a constitutive function for the structure of obsessional neurosis, but that is not, as such, distinctive of obsessional neurosis. We can see this as an updated version of Freud's notion of the "choice of neurosis", where the different types of neurosis are seen as the outcome of a particular relation to the libidinal satisfaction of the drive (Freud, 1913i, p. 318).

The important difference is that by introducing the term "desire" Lacan also introduces a fundamental reference to the Other, and the idea that it is the relation to the desire *of the Other* that has a structurally constitutive function for all the neuroses. For Lacan, obsessional neurosis and hysteria are thus both defined by the different ways they relate to the desire of the Other as the "place of desire" as such: "the locus in which desire, or the possible formulation of desire, has to be discovered" (Lacan, 1957–1958, p. 384). Although this place of desire is not solely or exclusively constitutive of the obsessional structure, it is the point in relation to which obsessional neurosis articulates itself and finds its own specific "formulation of desire," the point from where the obsessional structure is articulated in its specificity and difference from the structure of hysteria.

The other way in which Lacan uses the idea of "relationship to desire" refers more specifically to the orientation of obsessional neurosis towards a particular way of desiring, towards a specific "formulation of desire" which marks its structural difference from hysteria. Lacan talks in this sense about a "centre of gravity" in the movement of hysteria and obsessional neurosis (ibid., p. 379). Here Lacan retains from Freud not only the idea of a *field* of forces, where desire and satisfaction gravitate towards particular points or objects, but also the idea of a *fixation* which becomes constitutive of the choice of neurosis. This is the point which Lacan insists on more, possibly because the subject's fixation and gravitation towards a certain type of desire is what is most palpable in clinical practice, whereas the primary relationship to the desire of the Other is something that is implicit and only retroactively reconstructed from it, as Leclaire's case will illustrate. In general, we could say that Lacan suggests that if the relation to the desire of the Other is what *constitutes* the structure, the relationship to a particular type of desire is what *manifests* the basic and distinctive articulation of the structure.

The centre of gravity of obsessional neurosis

Readers of Lacan are familiar with the many different facets and types of desire described by Lacan. A well-known Italian Lacanian analyst, Massimo Recalcati, has counted them off in a very imaginative way in a recent best-selling book, *Portraits of Desire* (*Ritratti del Desiderio*; Recalcati, 2012), written as a kind of guided tour through a gallery of portraits, each chapter corresponding to a particular portrait or aspect of desire from Lacan's teaching: envious desire, the desire of the Other, anxious desire, the desire for nothing, the desire to enjoy, romantic desire, sexual desire, the desire for death, pure desire and, finally, the desire of the analyst. The type of desire that provides the centre of gravity for obsessional neurosis is described by Lacan as "desire in a pure state", as an "absolute condition" that "negates" and "destroys" the Other by overriding everything else (Lacan, 1957–1958, pp. 37–80). This type of desire also manifests the basic articulation of the obsessional structure. Lacan writes down this basic structural articulation as $d0$, where "0" stands for zero, the effect of negation of the obsessional's desire on the Other, and more precisely on the desire of the Other (ibid., p. 442). Conversely, hysteria is defined by its gravitation towards the desire of the Other. The basic structural articulation of hysteria is thus written by Lacan as dx, where "x" stands for the hysteric's question regarding the desire of the Other (ibid., p. 442).

As often, Lacan is very keen on showing that what he says can be rigorously traced back to Freud. In this case, he points to a passage from *The Ego and the Id* where Freud introduces the idea of a "defusion of the intrication of instincts" in obsessional neurosis (Freud, 1923b, p. 41). According to Freud, the life and death drive are intricated, fused together, but in obsessional neurosis there is an early desintrication or defusion of the death drive that marks the developmental trajectory of the obsessional. The "desire in a pure state" of the obsessional mentioned by Lacan, therefore, is connected to the death drive and to the way this is originally defused, desintricated from the life drive in the obsessional.

Lacan further explains both the pure and the destructive character of the obsessional's desire in the light of the symbolic dialectic of need, demand and desire that he elaborates throughout *Seminar V*. He situates pure desire "beyond demand", that is, beyond what can be asked or expected from the Other by a subject (Lacan, 1957–1958, p. 361). For Lacan, as long as we are *asking* – asking for the satisfaction of a need, for a sign of love or for a sign of presence or recognition – we are at the level of demand and within a register where the Other remains the primary reference. When we start to *desire* something, however, and particularly if we want it regardless of any need and, most importantly, regardless also of what anybody may say or do about the fact that we want it, then we are at a different level: at the level of pure desire, beyond demand, where the Other, as Lacan puts it, "loses its predominance" (ibid., p. 361). Desire thus emerges in its most pure and absolute form as a leftover, as a remainder from what can be asked and expected from the Other. Its destructive character lies in the way it has to negate and annul the Other as a point of address in order to constitute itself in this way.

Lacan gives a striking example of how the obsessional gravitates towards this particular aspect of desire by inviting his audience to consider the case of the little child "who is going to become an obsessional" and who wants a box, a little box – the case of the little obsessional who asks for a little box (that is, for nothing, really) and becomes totally fixated on it (ibid., p. 379). The little box is clearly not requested as an object of need or as a sign of love, and the pure and destructive quality of the child's desire in relation to the Other becomes manifest, according to Lacan, precisely in the way his parents – the Other – would typically find this fixation completely intolerable. In front of the child's fixation with getting the box at all cost, anything that the parent-Other may say or do disappears: the child's desire annuls the parent-Other, whose irritation at the child makes this apparent.

The obsessional and the internal contradiction of desire

After isolating in $d0$ (desire annuls the Other) the basic structural articulation of obsessional neurosis, Lacan tries to show how the most distinctive problems that the obsessional manifests in the clinic can be traced back to this fundamental articulation. In line with the psychoanalytic literature of his time, Lacan first considers how the destructive tendency of the obsessional's desire can be observed clinically at the level of the cruel and sadistic fantasies which overwhelm the obsessional's psychic life. Lacan points out, however, that the obsessional does not enter analysis to talk about his fantasies but to talk about his "impediments, inhibitions, barriers, fears, doubts and prohibitions" (ibid., p. 389). He has a distinctive relation to his sadistic fantasies which not only excludes that they should be ever realised, but which also makes it hard for him to confess and talk about them. Why?

Lacan examines a first explanation, which he identifies with the object-relation approach: the obsessional's difficulty in acting on and even confessing to his fantasies is caused by the fear that the other would return his aggression, by the "fear of himself undergoing destruction equivalent to that of the desire he displays" (ibid., p. 393). Lacan does not reject this explanation, but considers it insufficient insofar as it is centred on the imaginary register of specular aggression and rivalry, and it does not acknowledge how the relation between the subject and the Other is also organised symbolically by the signifier.

For Lacan, the crux of the obsessional's difficulties in his relationship to desire is elsewhere. The problem is not so much that the obsessional's desire is inhibited by the fear of retaliation from the Other, but rather that the obsessional has a peculiar difficulty in keeping his desire going, in maintaining and sustaining it. The cause of this difficulty is structural, not imaginary, and boils down to an internal contradiction which belongs to the structure of desire as such. On the one hand, each subject wants to realise himself through his desire – "the desire to have one's desire" as separate from the desire of the Other (ibid., p. 407). On the other hand, however, the only place where the subject can look for and find his desire is the desire of the Other, which is the "place of desire" as such (ibid., p. 381).

Lacan presents this as a contradiction that concerns every speaking subject, but also shows us that this contradiction becomes particularly apparent and sensitive for the obsessional, precisely because of the way in which the obsessional gravitates towards the "the desire to have one's desire" and towards a form of desire which negates and annuls the Other. The obsessional, as we have seen, affirms his desire by a particular way of asking which annuls and destroys the Other. In doing so, however, he also annuls any possible reference to the desire of the Other, which is the very place and source of desire, and thus sees his own desire fade and falter each time he tries to realise it.

Clinically, this contradiction can be observed in the obsessional's distinctive relation towards his objects. Typically, the obsessional would concentrate his desire on a particular object, as in the little box example quoted above. The closer the obsessional gets to obtain this object, however, the more the object would become worthless, just a piece of nothing, since in obtaining what he wants the obsessional simultaneously loses the reference to the desire of the Other which is necessary to sustain desire and to confer value to any object. Lacan captures the logic of the obsessional's struggle to keep his desire alive through a reference to the mythological figure of Tantalus. Hungry and thirsty, Tantalus was condemned by the Gods to a punishment that consisted in standing immersed in the waters of a lake with an apple tree extending its branches over him. As soon as Tantalus reached out to pick an apple, the branches of the tree would move away, and as soon as he lowered his head to drink the water of the lake the water would lower and prevent him from drinking.

More generally, the operation of negation of the Other which constitutes the obsessional's desire also confers to the obsessional's desire its distinctive mortifying character. In the book I referred to earlier, Massimo Recalcati devotes particular attention to this point and shows that when desire emancipates itself from any reference to the desire of the Other it also naturally tends to manifest itself as a perpetually unsatisfied desire, as a *desire for something else* that discards any possible object of satisfaction, and ultimately also as a *desire for nothing* and a *desire for death*. Recalcati uses the figure of Mozart's Don Giovanni to illustrate the mortifying drift of desire disconnected from the desire of the Other. Don Giovanni is a figure of pure desire who demands and expects nothing from the Other. His desire negates the Other and transcends demand because it is always desire for something else, for one woman after another, for nothing that may actually exist or be granted to him, but for this very reason eventually also desire for nothing itself, desire for death.

Oblativity and symptom formation

Lacan's next step in *Seminar V* is to show how the obsessional tries to deal with the impasse brought about by his relationship to desire by way of a specific symptomatic solution. If a symptomatic solution is a compromise between defence and satisfaction, the logic underpinning the symptomatic solution of the obsessional involves, we could say, an appeal to the Other, an appeal through which the obsessional can prevent some of the mortifying effects of his negation of the Other, while at the same time maintaining his orientation towards a desire which negates the Other.

The obsessional manages to achieve this compromise through a sleight of hand which consists in separating the Other who desires from the Other who demands. Lacan observes how the obsessional is "always in the process of asking permission" and highlights how "to the very extent that the dialectic with the Other is called into question, challenged and even put in danger" asking permission is ultimately a way to "apply oneself to restoring this Other" (Lacan, 1958–1959, p. 390). Crucially, however, the Other that is restored by the obsessional is not the Other of desire, but the Other of demand, the Other who makes demands of the subject. This is the Other of the rule, of the request, of the prohibition and of the permission, but also the Other of the technical procedure and of the measurement, a completely rational and consistent Other who has no desire. The obsessional tries to make this version of the Other exist, appeals to it continuously and submits himself completely to it. The technical terms for this symptomatic strategy is "oblativity" – a term which indicates a complete submission to the demands of the Other and which originally referred to the offering of a gift or action to the Gods.

Oblativity functions as a symptomatic compromise because, on the one hand, it is just one of the ways in which the obsessional can continue to destroy and annul the Other. By submitting to the Other of demand the obsessional destroys the Other of desire and reduces the Other to a dead set of rules and procedures. His orientation of desire is thus preserved and the obsessional can still affirm his own desire through an act of submission which is truly only a way of annulling and disregarding Other. On the other hand, however, oblativity also protects the obsessional against the fading away of desire which the destruction of the place of desire in the Other entails, since the logic of prohibition allows him to maintain and keep his desire alive as an impossible desire, as something kept at a distance by the demands and rules imposed by the Other.

This logic of oblativity underpins many of the symptomatic formations of the obsessional. If we look at Freud's case of the Rat Man, for example, the rules and prohibitions that the Rat Man sets up for himself can be seen as an example of this consistent Other of demand. In his presentation of the case, Freud already highlighted how the Rat Man's obsessive thoughts took the form of logically structured "sanctions" (*"that he was not to pay back the money* or it would happen – (that is, the fantasy about the rats would come true as regards his father and the lady)") and that these sanctions had their roots in the Rat Man's infantile fear that something terrible would befall the people he loved (and more specifically his father) if he had given in to his sexual compulsions (Freud, 1909d, pp. 166–168). Lacan's theory allows us to see that the Rat Man's infantile fear stemmed from an intuition of the inherently destructive effect of his desire on the Other. Through Lacan, besides, it is also possible to grasp the subtle symptomatic compromise at play in the oblativity of the Rat Man's "sanctions", where the Other is at once destroyed (i.e., reduced to a mere logical formula) and restored *qua* verbal sanction, as a barrier against the destructive effect of desire. Lacan refers to this logic as an "articulated destruction" of the Other, where "it is only with a particular articulation of signifiers that the obsessional subject manages to preserve the Other, so much so that the effect of destruction is also the means by which he aspires to sustain it by virtue of the articulation of signifiers" (Lacan, 1958–1959, pp. 444, 446).

Serge Leclaire and the Philo case

The case of Philo, presented by Serge Leclaire for the *Evolution Psychiatrique* group in 1958 under the title: "Philo, or the obsessional and his desire", provides a unique clinical illustration of the structural approach to obsessional neurosis developed by Lacan in *Seminar V*. Leclaire followed and collaborated very closely with Lacan throughout the 1950s and 1960s and the case works in many ways as a complement to Lacan's teaching on obsessional neurosis.

In the original text of the case published shortly after Lacan's seminar, we can see Leclaire trying to apply Lacan's ideas to his clinical work and engaging in a direct dialogue with Lacan. Lacan comments on Leclaire's work in the way I have outlined above, highlighting the importance of Leclaire's focus on those clinical details where the "universal signification of desire" emerges. Lacan's remark is precious to appreciate the method followed by Leclaire. Leclaire proceeds by drawing out the crucial moments when the question of the desire of the Other – the "universal signification of desire" in Lacan's phrase – comes up, both in the transference and in the subject's speech, both as a re-enactment of the subject's confrontation with this question in the relationship with the analyst and as a fixation of the signification of desire in particular details of the subject's history. In this way, Leclaire's case study provides much more than a simple illustration of Lacan's ideas and actually shows how the basic articulation of obsessional neurosis isolated by Lacan – $d0$ – is played out at different levels in the subject's history and in the position he comes to occupy in the transference.

Philo is described by Leclaire as a bachelor close to the age of thirty, with the problem of not knowing what to do with his life and "three main passions": rejecting the advice he repeatedly seeks, having someone love him and failing in a task (Leclaire, 1958, pp. 114f). From the start, Leclaire opts to say little about Philo's history and to centre his presentation around a "fragment of his discourse" instead (ibid., p. 115). The fragment is reported almost *verbatim* by Leclaire and contains, embedded in a short interjection uttered by Philo in a burst of rage, a minute revelatory detail which shows up the most reduced and minimal articulation of Philo's obsessional structure. Philo is talking about his very close bond with his mother. Leclaire asks him to say more about how this bond was formed and this triggers a very sudden aggressive outburst against the analyst, unusual for a patient otherwise extremely poised and civilised. Philo bursts out with this sentence addressed to Leclaire: *"Merde! Comme si ça te regardait!"* (ibid., p. 116). This sentence has two different meanings in French: "Shit! It is none of your business!" and, more literally, "Shit! It is not looking at you!"

The ambiguity – which plays on the literal and metaphorical meanings of the verb *regarder* in French (to look at; to concern) – is crucial because Philo then goes on to explain to Leclaire that the close bond with his mother started *from her eyes*, in which he thought he could see how she was finding in him the satisfaction she could not find in his father and how this made him necessary to her. More precisely, Philo describes how he believed he was able to see his mother's desire for him as a "second gaze", contained within his mother's gaze (ibid., p. 116). Starting from this exchange of looks, Philo developed what he describes as a symbiosis, a "secret complicity" with his mother, and felt that the unique goal of his life was to be necessary to his mother and to do what she wanted, becoming "her slave and her master at the same time" (ibid., p. 116).

The place of desire in the case

The detail isolated by Leclaire – the mother's gaze – identifies the desire of the Other and thus the "place" of desire as such – the point where the "universal signification of desire" emerges in the case as something separate from but also articulated with the "particular" relation to this point which marks Philo's subjective position. Philo's description of his mother's gaze is the description of his encounter with the desire of the Other, in relation to which he is called to define and find his own desire. The structural key, the "navel" of the case here is Philo's description of the "second gaze" within his mother's gaze. Philo's obsessional neurosis, his "essential and resistant difficulty", as Leclaire puts it, has its point of fixation in his belief that he can see what the Other wants in the emptiness of the Other's gaze. From the moment Philo thinks he can catch a glimpse of himself as his mother's object of desire, from the moment the place of desire in his mother's eyes is closed down by a representation of Philo as his mother's phallus, rather than being kept open by a phallic signification of its emptiness, Philo's obsessional trajectory and his obsessional difficulties with desire are set.

Leclaire inscribes this exchange of looks rigorously in the oedipal model set out by Lacan and backs it up with biographical material from the case. Philo, we find out, had since childhood idealised and wished to emulate "Gonzago-who-died-a-martyr-among-the-barbarians", a heroic ancestor of his father. Philo's mother, on the other hand, had loved Philo's father for his descendance from the same dead family hero, who had been her true secret love. Through identification with Gonzago, Philo had thus been able to see himself as the phallic object of his mother's desire in his mother's gaze – at the cost, however, of failing to acknowledge his father as the external reference of his mother's desire and the paternal phallus as the signification of his mother's desire. Because he experienced his mother's satisfaction, rather than dissatisfaction, Philo remains stuck in the position of being his mother's imaginary phallus, and never quite gets to the point where he may receive a symbolic phallus from his father and access a desiring position as a subject in the register of having (a career, money, a woman, etc.).

Consistently with Freud's original idea, Leclaire in this way anchors Philo's obsessional structure in a premature libidinal excess of satisfaction. This excess of satisfaction is condensed in the "second" gaze which Philo's tries to grasp and sees in his mother's "first" gaze. If the "second gaze" provides the point of fixation for Philo's fantasy, the articulation between Philo's gaze on one side, and his mother's "first" and "second" gaze on the other provides the fundamental structural articulation of obsessional neurosis itself. This is precisely what Lacan writes as "$d0$", the negation of the desire of the Other nested in the mother's first gaze annulled and masked by the fantasy of the precious phallic status that Philo wants to believe he has for his mother. In this respect, it is striking to see how Leclaire's presentation shows that all the structural coordinates of obsessional neurosis set out by Lacan in *Seminar V* can already be found in this minimal but fundamental articulation, and that, once this crucial nexus is identified, the same articulation offers a unique and recognisable structuring principle for the rest of the material.

For example, the distinctive orientation of the obsessional towards a desire that annuls and destroys the Other is implicit in Philo's attempt to see his own desire reflected in a "second" gaze contained within his mother's "first" gaze. The "second" gaze destroys the Other, makes his father redundant and annuls the signification of the desire of the Other hidden in the emptiness of his mother's "first" gaze. This can also be found more explicitly in the aggressive remark addressed to the analyst ("Shit! This is none of your business!/it is not looking at you!") who has, in the transference, and by making his own "fourth" gaze appear on the scene, unveiled the signification of desire in the mother's "first" gaze, and threatened the fantasy that Philo wants to be able to read in it as a "second" gaze. The "first" version of the mother's gaze as the place of desire can of course only be reconstructed after the fact. It does, however, reappear again and again in the case, fraught with anxiety and incarnated in other successive versions of it encountered each time Philo is confronted with the mystery of a living, desiring Other: not only in Philo's persistent discomfort in front of the analyst's opaque gaze, but also, for instance, in a dream where he punches to a pulp the face of a man who stares insistently, and inexplicably, at him.

The other distinctive structural trait highlighted by Lacan – the obsessional's difficulty in sustaining his desire – is also contained in the minimal articulation of this scene. Philo's glimpse of the "second gaze" is also precisely what destroys what can sustain his desire: the reference to the desire of the Other as the place of desire itself and the phallus *qua* signification of desire. Leclaire refers from the start to Philo's general problem of not knowing what to do with his life. Many other details from the case also illustrate this point. Philo's wilful ignorance of the Other as a being of desire, for example, reduces all his partners to the status of shadows that disappoint him as soon as he touches them. He experiences the world as from behind a "glass shell" (ibid., p. 114). Trapped within the sterile fantasy of his communion with his mother, he is unable to desire by assuming the position of someone who has the phallus: at thirty years old he doubts his manliness, he can't decide on his career, he feels like a child, he is not quite ready to have a woman "like the other men" and he "almost hears a voice who tells him 'when you grow up…'" (ibid., p. 123).

The characteristic symptomatic formation of the obsessional – oblativity – is contained in a similar way in the scene. The articulation "first gaze"/"second gaze" is an example of the "articulated destruction" which Lacan refers to in his discussion of oblativity. Philo sees one version of the Other in his mother's eyes – the master he wants to make himself necessary to – and by doing this he destroys another Other – the living Other of desire glimpsed in the emptiness of his mother's gaze. The material of the case provides ample illustration of this logic. Philo allows himself not only "the privilege of exposing his doubts to whoever wants to listen to them" but also, and most of all, "the privilege of disputing the other's decisions" (ibid., p. 115). He is constantly caught up in the act of creating what Leclaire refers to as a "fantasy Other that provides an illusory support to his sterile desire" (ibid., p. 127). He has a propensity for spectacular failure, for exposing his flaws and his ignorance to others as a way of invoking an Other who may eventually help him to escape his predicament, but who is actually yet another lifeless fictional Other incapable of granting him access to a different formulation of his desire.

Dismembering, desire, and psychoanalytic practice

Leclaire's case study on Philo could be compared to Freud's case studies for the way it demonstrates something essential about analytic practice. The words used by Lacan in *Seminar V* to describe Freud's method in his five famous case histories could easily be applied to Leclaire's work with Philo: just like Freud, Leclaire "works on the material to the point where the articulations that seem irreducible to him have been properly detached" and "constantly returns to rigorously examine the part that we can call the symbolic origin and the part that is the real origin, in the primitive chain of the subject's history" (Lacan, 1957–1958, p. 220). Leclaire himself seemed well aware of the paradigmatic quality of his account of Philo's analysis when he republished the case in a 1971 book, aptly titled *Unmasking the Real* [*Démasquer le réel*]. In this book Leclaire refers to his presentation of Philo's case as an example of how analytic practice proceeds by extracting such parts of "symbolic origin and real origin" from the subject's symbolic chain. The operation that exposes the "split" [*clivage*] and the "joint" between a real lack within the symbolic order and the fantasmatic representation of this lack – between the mother's "first gaze" and "second gaze" in Philo's case – is equated by Leclaire to analytic interpretation and to the productivity of a practice that unblocks the process of signification and undoes the subject's fixation to a particular representation of lack (Leclaire, 1971, pp. 26–29).

Beyond the many similarities between what Lacan and Leclaire have to say about obsessional neurosis, therefore, the significance of reading them together lies in the way Leclaire's case study illuminates how the "dismembering of obsessional neurosis" advocated by Lacan touches on psychoanalytic practice itself. Lacan's reference to Plato's image of the good butcher who can expertly detach the limbs of a body at their joints risks to pass as a metaphor for philosophical thought, or, at any rate, for a type of thought which proceeds systematically, by dissecting its object of enquiry in order to master any gap and lack in understanding. Although Lacan's highly theoretical formulations on obsessional neurosis in *Seminar V*, if read superficially, might compound this misconception, Leclaire's presentation of Philo's case shows how Lacan actually distances analytic practice from philosophical thought and how "dismembering" and "segmenting" are not used by Lacan as metaphors for any kind of thought. In fact, if "dismembering" referred merely to the activity of thought it would truly amount to little more than an obsessional symptom. It would be a form of "articulated destruction" of the Other, which would obscure, rather than reveal and detach, the fundamental joint between articulated thought and the place of desire in the Other, the place where articulated thought meets something real and heterogeneous to itself.

We could say then that Leclaire shows that in Lacan's approach "dismembering" is much less an attribute of thinking than of desiring, that it manifests not the activity of thought but the effect of desire as the driving force of analytic practice. If Lacan insists on how desire tends towards a veiled phallic signification of lack which escapes any particular signification, in his work with Philo Leclaire shows that desire is necessary to dismember and detach the articulation between the empty place of the desire of the Other and the fixed signification of fantasy through which the obsessional subject tries to fill the emptiness of desire and annul the Other. In *Démasquer le réel* Leclaire claims that it is "absolutely necessary" for an analyst to "know how to hold on to the phallic function" in order to "let go of the representations that come in the place of the object to feed the fantasy" and in order to "support the subject in his or her division" (ibid., p. 41). Considering the thread, we have followed from Lacan's *Seminar V* to Leclaire's Philo case we could add that the importance of this ability of the analyst to "hold on to desire" is not limited to the analytic manoeuvre in the clinic but extends to all the aspects of analytic practice, including the practice of articulating theory (Lacan) and the practice of writing and constructing a case (Leclaire).

In general, it also seems important to mention how Leclaire's case also clarifies and illustrates an essential point about Lacan's structuralist approach. If taken in isolation, Lacan's reference to Plato's metaphor of the bad butcher may suggest that Lacan is initiating an approach that gives ontological consistency to the idea of structure in psychoanalysis, and that the analyst's task is merely that of finding the articulations of the structure behind their clinical manifestations. Leclaire's work shows, however, that the psychoanalyst does not look for the "natural articulations" as the good butcher in Plato's dialogue is supposed to do. Philo's case demonstrates very clearly not only that the fundamental structural articulation can only be found by unveiling a point *outside* the structure, but also that the structure itself is constituted by the subject *from* and *in relation to* this external point where the subject is confronted with the desire of the Other. While the consistency of the structure remains in this way only logical in Lacan's approach, what is really brought to the fore is the way desire becomes essential to unravel the structure in the clinic. The effect of Leclaire's gaze on Philo (*"Merde! Comme si ca te regardait!"*) shows that desire must circulate as something living and real in the transference to allow for the fundamental articulation of the structure to emerge, repeat itself and ultimately manifest not only its necessity, but also its contingency in the process of analysis.

References

Freud, S. (1909d). Notes upon a case of obsessional neurosis. *S. E.*, *10*: 151–318. London: Hogarth, 1955.

Freud, S. (1913i). The disposition to obsessional neurosis. *S. E.*, *12*: 311–326. London: Hogarth, 1957.

Freud, S. (1923b). *The Ego and the Id*. *S. E.*, *19*: 1–66. London: Hogarth, 1961.

Lacan, J. (1957–1958). *The Seminar of Jacques Lacan, Book V, Formations of the Unconscious*. J.-A. Miller (Ed.), R. Grigg (Trans.). Cambridge: Polity, 2017.

Lacan, J. (1959). Discussion à la suite de l'exposé de Serge Leclaire "L'obsessionel et son désir". *Evolution Psychiatrique*, *3*: 409–411.

Leclaire, S. (1958). Philo, or the obsessional and his desire. In: S. Schneiderman (Ed. and Trans.). *Returning to Freud: Clinical Psychoanalysis in the School of Lacan*. New Haven and London: Yale University Press, 1980, pp. 114–129.

Leclaire, S. (1971). *Démasquer le réel. Un essai sur l'objet en psychanalyse*. Paris: Seuil.

Plato (1952). *Phaedrus*. R. Hackforth (Trans.). Cambridge: Cambridge University Press.

Recalcati, M. (2012). *Ritratti del desiderio*. Milano: Raffaello Cortina.

CHAPTER FIVE

The signification of mastery of the control of the orifices in anal eroticism[1]

MOUSTAPHA SAFOUAN

P sychoanalysts have located the moment when the subject becomes devoted to an ideal of mastery in the anal phase. But rather than wondering why the signification of mastery would *attach itself to* the exercise of a physiological function, i.e., the control of the sphincters, they believed that this bodily exercise *was in itself* the source of the signification in question.

Well, a dog that has been trained is still a dog. What I mean is that an organic function cannot draw meaning from itself, and certainly cannot endow our acts with meaning; only a fantasy, or a hastily constructed theory – in other words, a subject – has this capability. We are going to show in what follows that it is because of links between desire and the law that the excretory functions are transformed into behaviours in which mastery is symbolised. In the process, we hope to some extent to elucidate both the signification of the mastery and the nature of the links.

***

The reader will doubtless recall the Rat Man's recounting of the rat torture to Freud, which he was unable to do without his face showing "horror at pleasure of his own of which he himself was unaware" (Freud, 1909d, p. 167).

Let us imagine another story in which the victim could choose to have this torture carried out on him: "There were so many prisoners in China that the prisons were overflowing. In order to get rid of some of them, they were given the following choice: either to stay in prison for the rest of their life, or to take a rat and push it into their rectum."

Judging by the effect this story produces when I tell it, while it might amuse an audience, there is nothing about it that would banish the phantom of jouissance.

From this we can deduce the following:

1.   the Rat Man imagined the anal region of his own body to be the locus of a jouissance that was essentially the Other's jouissance of him; and that this Other could not, however, obtain jouissance from him without taking him by force, raping him, and treating him like a mere sack.
2.   it was the idea that the Other obtained jouissance, or wished to obtain it from him in this way, i.e., *maliciously*, which ultimately caused his own jouissance.

With regard to a phantasmatic constraint which would annul his will, the obsessional's choices (because to this day the Rat Man remains the most exemplary case of obsessional neurosis) could only be a defence, an avoidance or a systematic distancing of this very jouissance, the spectre of which constantly haunts him. The mastery of motility certainly has meaning, but it is not power or the will to power; it is rather the means of protecting the subject from a jouissance by which he feels controlled. This is something we need to explain.

***

Let us imagine a subject for whom the only motivation for any sort of action is a challenge; without being challenged to do something, he would not only be disorientated but completely lacking orientation. In this we can surely recognise the obsessional. But what do we mean by a challenge?

A challenge sometimes seems like rivalry: "I challenge you to lift this weight." But this apparent similarity dissipates when we observe that rivalry proper is a competition expressly accepted by the rivals, in relation to a given object: a prize, a job, not to mention the women around whom rivalries are often socially organised. The chance of winning is not impossible in principle for either of the rivals; which in turn means that the rival is a fellow-creature: he could also lose.

It is quite another matter where rivalry of, shall we say, an intimate variety is concerned, that is to say undeclared rivalry, which animated the Rat Man in relation to "these gentlemen the professional officers"; or again the rivalry the mere presence of his cousin Dick sufficed to unleash in him, to the point of arousing a mortifying tension which was turned in on himself in a quasi-suicidal form. The difference is such that we cannot say in a rigorous way that the Rat Man was rivalrous: for him, rivalry was just a sickness.

So, what exactly is this morbid rivalry? And who (or what) are these rivals, who are as many as they are mute? Freud's reply was as follows: they are repetitions of the father. In other words, he discovered that this rivalry is mediated, the rival, unlike in the animal kingdom, being defined by something more than a mere gestalt. So how does this mediation come about?

This question is closely linked to that of the challenge. Indeed, the challenge properly defined (for example: "I challenge you to oust me", or "to prove what you are saying") presupposes an *other* will besides my own (in this case the will to oust me) and at the same time a "law". One will is articulated as a demand: "Go away!", "Admit the truth!" (i.e., the truth which I choose to impute to you, for example your lie or your plagiarism). And I call it a "law" (in inverted commas) because this demand is presented as a commandment which this will imposes, or wishes to impose. The challenge supposes the Other in so far as he dictates his law, a law which is both arbitrary and capricious, and is fundamentally malicious; because it is not the law of any game, not even of a game such as the one that gave its name to a famous novel by Roger Vailland (1945), which, in so far as it is a game, implies at the very least the recognition of the partner as a human subject.

Let us now consider this unmotivated commandment, unmotivated to the extent that the search for its *raison d'être* has never ceased: "Thou shalt not sleep with thy mother". It is a demand, a demand that carries the weight of a commandment issuing from a will deemed to be that of a father. To this I can reply: "That is your desire. Personally, I refuse to allow such a limitation of mine." In this very reply, there it is, my own desire (which, by the way, is mine only in so far as it is the desire to be the object of the mother's desire, in other words, it is anything but free), there it is being transfigured into a desire to make the law in its own turn: there we can see it "seduced by the commandment".[2]

To put it another way, the very form of a commandment, evincing the presence of the figure of the lawmaker, is enough to arouse the wish to be this lawmaker; it is a wish so powerful it knows no limits – it is fair to say that – and the satisfaction of it resides precisely in the belief in its object. Is it necessary to undergo the experience of analysis in order to realise that there would be no reason to believe in God, other than for the function assigned to Him by Descartes as the creator of eternal truths?

In this genesis, it is thus a question of a necessity reinforced by circumstances: notably when the one presumed to be the legislator, having himself been seduced by the commandment, tends to conform to the appearance of the lawmaker, or when his word proves to have no more authority with the mother than that of a fellow-being or a brother: that is to say, none whatsoever, since for once the mother personifies the law. What disappears in all cases is the manifestation of the law in so far as it is situated outside the realm of the will, or its manifestation as the law of the will in the objective sense and not in the subjective sense of the genitive. And from then on, what can the subject do – let us not speak of the child any more – except become committed to putting others on the wrong scent, if he cannot give satisfaction?

"If he cannot give satisfaction"! In truth, as far as satisfying the fundamentally servile wellspring of desire, there is simply no question of it, even if the subject had the means; especially if he had the means. In other words, the subject has no choice but to take on, or as we say, to internalise, the commandment, without this internalisation in any way resolving the fundamental, constitutive discordance between his desire and the law. Even more, the internalisation reinforces the discordance while at the same time concealing it. The more the subject takes on all sorts of laws, written or unwritten, the more guilty he feels, quite incomprehensibly: for this taking on of the law is precisely the only effective way he can satisfy his desire to make the law.[3]

Furthermore, the revolt that ensued when a Nobel laureate of our century tried to find the human face that conforms to the law of pleasing others, was just as powerless as conformism is to shake the general submission to the law of pleasing; for desire remains its slave in (and through) its very discordance with the law.

The more the subject, following the law of pleasing, phantasmatically localises the jouissance of the Other in a part of his own body, the less he will be able to extricate the act – which on occasion

might bring him some satisfaction – from his powerlessness in relation to the fantasy (or more exactly, from the anxiety regarding his
powerlessness).

***

From then on, his relations with his fellow-beings will be enlivened by
a rivalry of "pure prestige", or to put it more exactly and more truth-
fully, a rivalry with the aim of losing. And what is the latest thing that
analysts are hearing? That analysands are amazed to find themselves
driven by rivalry for objects they do not even want!

At the heart of this rivalry we find the desire for mastery, or the
desire to do things only if I desire them, with my empty desire, which
is tantamount to saying that it is the desire to be the origin of the discourse. It is a desire which, for us, defines the "murder of the father"
and is a sign of it.

Indeed, just as foreclosure of the Name-of-the-Father echoes in the
Imaginary of a Schreber through "soul murder", so the repression of the
Name-of-the-Father echoes in the image of the corpse. In the phenomenology of obsessional neurosis this image occupies such a prominent
place that it has led certain analysts to emphasise what they call the
relation of the obsessional to death, which in fact is nothing other than
the imaginary effect of an unresolved relation to castration. It is unresolved in the following sense: the obsessional clings to the notion of the
one exception, that of the master. The master in whom he believes so
firmly that, as far as the obsessional's relation to death is concerned, it
can be summed up thus: he does not believe in it.

The basis of everything, then, is "he does not know" which, according to Lacan's graph, defines the subject at the level of enunciation:
that is to say, of ignorance, not of the distinction between the forbidden object and the permitted object (the *dictum* "no-one is supposed to
be ignorant of the law" could be well placed in an anthology of black
humour on the subject of any law except that prohibiting incest) but, if
I can put it this way, ignorance of the fact that: I can only live because
I am mortal; or again: that the father is not the origin of discourse.
"The law of desire", in the subjective sense of the genitive, is a piece
of "evidence" which deludes consciousness straight away. But because
of this, the "objective" sense of the genitive, if we can put it that way,
only re-asserts its rights more tyrannically: since the heart of the fellow-
being remains inhabited by malevolence, which leaves the subject no

alternative but to defend himself with a final refusal which he can so easily mistake for "self-mastery".

And since the subject has not given up wondering, either, about the heart of the Other, which he dreads as being the locus of Sadean jouissance,[4] without recognising in it the malevolence in his own heart, there is a possible basis for analysis and its termination. Whereas if we reduce the mastery of motility to a will to power, with all that implies when the relations between subjects are regarded as a power struggle, we situate analysis in an impasse before we even begin.

In the same way, we will not be able to lighten the burdens the subject bears by referring to the myth of Oedipus, because the myth is the locus where thought can recuperate a jouissance for which the subject has lost all opportunity. If we proceed in that direction, all we will achieve is to manage the anxiety that would arise if the subject (whether ourselves or our analysand) were led to the point of realising that nothing that he considers doing is actually forbidden to him, and if he were to be invited, through that realisation, to let go of a mastery which should not be confused with true discipline.

Notes

1. Taken from a seminar given during 1968–1969 on "The avatars of debt".
2. Cf., Epistle to the Romans, 7.
3. This is a paradox we touch on – we can do no more – when we see in certain instances some analysts insisting on placing their own function under the sign they call being "the guarantor of the law", without any notion of how ridiculous this is. To the point where one might wonder if this reference to the law is as essential to them as is the belief for a doctor that he or she is a "good" doctor.
4. This is expressed in Lacan's well-known maxim in "Kant with Sade" (Lacan, 1966, pp. 645–668).

References

Freud, S. (1909d). Notes upon a case of obsessional neurosis. *S. E., 10*: 151–318. London: Hogarth, 1955.

Lacan, J. (1966). *Écrits*. B. Fink (Trans.). New York: Norton, 2002.

Vailland, R. (1945). *Drôle de jeu* [*Playing with Fire*]. G. Hopkins (Trans.). London: Chatto & Windus, 1948.

CHAPTER SIX

The Rat Man[1]

CHARLES MELMAN

Our Association (Association lacanienne internationale) has once again taken up a theme that is dear to me, and I cannot thank them enough. But I should explain that the aspect of the theme that is dear to me is the following: quite incontestably, Freud's observations on the subject constitute the Rosetta Stone of psychoanalysis, and it seems that a great deal remains to be deciphered, for very good reasons connected with what we call the work of thinking – with what functions for each one of us as the work of thinking.

What, for example, do we do when we have to prepare to give a paper? Of course, we place the object to be covered by the paper in the field of representations – where else would we put it? We try to keep a reasonable distance, neither too near nor too far away. We start by listing the formulations which, at the time of the presentation of our own study, have already been put forward. And on that basis, we produce our own, however original or not it may be relative to those already produced within the parameters prescribed. And indeed, whatever we are going to say on the subject is already there, virtually, before we give voice to it. What we call the process of thinking is already mistaken, because *a priori* our work will consist in suturing whatever our own relation is to an object of study which is fundamentally (if it is truly an object of study) cut off from the field of perception.

As you know, in the Rat Man, the women who seduce him are *"Näherinnen"* – *"näher"* meaning "nearer", "closer by", *"die Näherin"* meaning the seamstress, the one who brings together the two extremities of the "lips", of the cut, of the suture – his objects are systematically *"Näherinnen"*. I know you'll say, "Oh, there goes Melman again! Just the sort of thing he would say! That's his 'thesis'!" It is an interpretation which seems to me to be rather difficult to refute, and yes, it is my thesis. Except that in the Rat Man case the other woman who is the object of his desire is his female cousin! We are forever having to re-do the stitching!

So, do we not find ourselves here in what I call the extraordinary garden of miracles in which the obsessional disports himself? He thought he was doing the right thing, he was trying to solve a major problem – the fact that there is a lack in the Other! And it is quite obvious that the primordial Other for him is his mama, his mother, and that it is a question of finding a remedy, a way of compensating for this lack in the Other which in this case is primordially maternal.

On this basis, we can hardly be surprised to find fully constituted obsessional neuroses in children of seven or eight years of age. And they are fully constituted, believe me: everything is there; and yet there is no sexual activity. I remember a little girl whose parents brought her to see me, because she was tormented by rituals that took up most of her time, and whose obsessional neurosis – it was all there – had been triggered by the death of her little brother. Given that it was not a question of the death of the father, how do you relate the appearance of obsessional neurosis in this little girl, her complete absorption by it, with the death of her little brother, in other words, the death of the obstacle to the perfection of her relation to the mother?

Zwangseinfall [obsessional idea]. *Der Zwang* [compulsion] is the pincers [*die Zange*] that trap and hold you in their jaws ... But what do they hold? They hold whatever will *"einfallen"* to you, whatever will occur to you, get into you. So, we are concerned with these jaws, this 1 and this 2, which hold on to something that is about to get into you, and from that moment on you cannot get rid of it. I will present it to you in the following manner so that you can feel its strange similarity with the introduction of the sexual, but which concerns the One of the phallus which you can only reject by means of foreclosure, and not through repression. And there, we are concerned with the object, the object *a* which, caught between S1 and S2, between these two jaws, ought to be expelled, yet finds itself stuck there, wedged between the two. At the same time, you no longer have any psychical means, any defence, against this intrusion.

The odd thing is that obsessional neurosis presents itself just like paranoia – the subject is persecuted by whatever happens without ceasing, and has no defence against it. But it is linked, and the agent is not the One, the stranger, but the familiar object *a*, one of your own. What follows is that the injunctions that emanate from this object – because this object *a* is very loquacious, very talkative – does not refer to an at-least-one, but to an *a*+, if we can put it that way.

In our day-to-day thought processes, obsessional manifestations are commonplace. What I mean is that where you ought to declare your sorrow, it is quite easy for the wrong sort of thought to come into your mind. "Oh dear, he's ill, what a pity!" is replaced by, "Drop dead!". The problem is that this is the habitual, normal daily course of our thoughts: something comes into your mind, is imposed on you, you do not want it, you find it intolerable, it makes you realise how bad you are, but still it comes; and where does it come from? Precisely from this bad object which has been cut off and which, in the case I am talking about, you have the power to repress.

But actually, this is not true in the case of obsessional neurosis; for here, for a reason I could describe as mechanical, you cannot repress that object. You may try to keep it at a distance, but you simply cannot repress it, because there is no Other space in which to do it. The Other has remained in the continuous symbolic chain in this sort of line which stretches into infinity, and you situate what we will call the paternal agency in infinity, in a virtual infinity. And this creature, this agency in infinity, is in abeyance because it has not been fully recognised, honoured, or satisfied. You will never be able to gratify this agency, which has the right to complete jouissance; because if you gratify it, you will terminate it, annul it, kill it, and if you do not gratify it, you leave it in a state of abeyance.

To repay? Or not to repay? In any case, there is always a debt.

But the problem is that you can neither pay it nor not pay it.

I am not going to recapitulate what I have already tried to show in the course of these seminars,[2] because I am going to devote myself to a particular piece of work, namely the deciphering of this Rosetta

Stone constituted by Freud's case, which is a priceless document. I had thought this would be thrilling and exciting for our Association, but this is clearly not the case. Perhaps it is not the case because, as good obsessionals, we have to keep our distance, or at least try to maintain some distance, from the place where this object is located.

And yet there are plenty of fundamental phenomena in this case that are very strange: there are two letters that keep cropping up all the time, z and w. *Zwang, zwei, zwischen, Zwicker.* With regard to the latter, we call it a *lorgnon* [pince-nez]. But it wasn't his *lorgnon* he lost, it was his *Zwicker!* And if you say *"lorgnon"*, you've bungled it, that's the end of it: his *Zwicker* is the thing that is between the two, *zwischen* [between], that which goes between the two, between the two eyes – and indeed we do also call it a pince-nez. He lost the thing that constituted the object "gaze" between the two, that is what he lost! And he did not know whether he should lose it or not. He did not know if he should go looking for it or not. He had been granted an infantile scopic enjoyment, that is where he definitively got caught up – what he saw underneath his nannies' skirts was not the semblance; he had not admired shapes and outlines through a night-dress or a dressing-gown, oh no: he, as a child, had climbed underneath and what he saw ... Well, what was it he saw? He saw that the trappings were in place in order to bar parts of the scopic field for reasons of modesty. He saw what was not supposed to be seen, what was supposed to give life to the semblance, what was supposed to make the semblance desirable. And yet he saw it! From this point onwards, it is easy to see how the loss of what was there between the two, of what was left wedged between the two, between S1 and S2, left him in a state of hesitation: shall I go looking for it, or will one be given back to me? The risk of losing it, and then the perplexity he experienced at that moment of an impossible reimbursement, impossible because if he paid it back, that would be the end of the story.

This is why when we speak of the death of the father ... there is something fundamental, fantastical in the surprises you encounter in the Rat Man case, which is that ... you really are in *Hamlet*! There's the dead father wandering around, not on the battlements, for sure, but in the corridor, and he's about to rap on the door, *knock-knock*, and he's about to come in, and he is going to see what? His son, the son who is failing in his filial duty, who is in the process of masturbating, and the entire case unfolds between military scenes, in the place where he has to be the One in the service of the father, and then the little *jouisseur*, the one who is trying to act like papa, is going to keep hidden what he has to pay.

In *Hamlet*, there is also the scene with the rat behind the arras, when Rosencrantz and Guildenstern are there, and there's that rat running away! Isn't it surprising to see just how permanent such a scenario can be? Why the rat? Not only for the richness of the declensions of the word, but for the rat as the image of a piece of excrement endowed with a soul, with life! What better representation could there be of the obsessional himself, torn between what could be called, by way of metaphor, this bestiality, the unlimited satisfaction of his needs, and, on the other hand, a subject who is present, who protests, who argues, who seeks to defend himself.

Which shows us – what? I am going to linger on this – which shows us what I saw when I first visited the asylums. There were obsessionals on the wards who had been there for years, pure obsessionals, who were being treated as psychotics, some of whom were lobotomised, yes indeed, sometimes they tried to extract the bit that was too much! Why is an obsessional not a psychotic? Why did Lacan tell us that obsessionality was the true neurosis? Why is it the true neurosis? It is because the relation to castration, to the agency of the phallus, is perfectly established.

Is there any proof of this? Yes, there is, the following bears witness to it: when the Rat Man goes to the station to catch the train for Vienna, and the porter says to him, "Ten o'clock train, sir?" – well, we can see the sort of message he receives, which is by no means an injunction. Is it a message that aims at him as a "thou", a performative message which he has to act upon, which he ought to act upon? No, it is a message which insinuates, which raises questions, which leaves him space to deliberate. And in this case, because there is room for deliberation, he knows that it is what he ought to do, without protesting. Now, that is amazing! Either way, he receives a message from the Other in an inverted form, which is not direct, as injunctions are. And throughout the case you have the evidence that the subject is present, in the form of his attempts to defend himself against obsessional ideas: there he is, overwhelmed, terrorised by what is being uttered. But where do these words that impose themselves on him come from? Normally, their source is a supposed locus, which we know to be inhabited by the unconscious, and which in any case is supposed to be Other. Whereas in his case, it comes to him from a locus that he is able to keep at a distance, but which is nonetheless always in continuity with that of the field of representations.

I am going to conclude with both the cross-cap and the knot. If we take the cross-cap, we have to imagine the possibility of two things. On the one hand, the constitution of the cross-cap itself, in other words, a line of interpenetration which we know to be governed by the phallus. On the other hand, there is the idea of the cutting out of the disc that constitutes the object *a*, but which is supposed to remain somehow in a sort of proximity – but what sort? that is the question! – which would remain, which could not be found anywhere except in a knot, and not in a cross-cap. And we would need to discover geometric properties which would ensure that, in spite of this cut, there was continuity between this object and the bag constituted by the remainder of the cross-cap.

So, what we have is the presence of a crushed subject, terrorised by what comes to him not from a locus which is reputed to be empty, the locus of the Other, and from where the paternal message should come for him to interpret in an inverted form, and would take care of castration, but rather from a locus from where these injunctions etc. come to him.

You can find proof of this in the Rat Man case – I'm saying this off the cuff – where there is sexual union between the anuses of two women, Freud's mother and his wife, mediated, if I remember rightly, by a herring. Well, now! Really! That's quite a bloke-ish idea, really the type of thing a bloke would do, and then Freud goes and gets mixed up in it ... You see that thing that creates a sexual union between two women, and between one anus and another ... Why a herring, *Hering*? Here you have *Ring, hören* = hearing, and even *Herr, Herr Schmitt, Herr Langer*. It would no longer be the phallus disrupting the sexual union, then, but rather the object, which would now be capable of inserting itself between S1 and S2, because obviously it has been saved from its own lack through what constitutes a symmetrical jouissance of S1 through this object.

Anyway, no-one understands a thing about all those complications of the reimbursement, the woman, Lieutenant A, Lieutenant B – and in the end he's going to rob the good woman, etc., etc. The ordinary fantasy of the obsessional male is obviously to pay back a debt to a woman, because as a child one can think that the fact that this woman loved him meant that she had given her love to him. It is a question of paying it back to a woman so that she in turn can give it to you. That is the famous homosexuality of the Rat Man! Freud speaks endlessly of the obsessional's homosexuality, but it doesn't just concern a man. As a good obsessional, where an other is concerned, he can only wish for his death. Here we find ourselves in Schema L: any encounter with a fellow-being takes the form of ... "All right, mate?" And then: "Still with us, are you? Weren't you ill last time we met? Even so, you do look a bit tired ... "That's how thinking works! Just observe your thoughts throughout one day, and by the end of that day you run the risk of being rather alarmed! So, the obsessional's "homosexuality" is not quite what it seems. There is also his oblativity,[3] his sense of equality and fair shares, making sure the shares are correct to the last penny, even to the extent of having repaid a debt to a woman, so that she can then give it back to him.

Is this of any interest to us, other than as pathology? Yes, because it is our way of thinking, our way of living, our psychical suffering, our going astray, our certitude that there's no escape from it, no way out. So where does that leave us? It leaves us at the point where I make the effort to take a pen and a piece of paper and become a thinker. We are fascinated by the thinker's activity, and we are also sufficiently advanced in our story to know that the thinker's activity is catastrophic! The thinker's activity consists in taking a pen and a piece of paper and writing. But once you start writing you are led to isolate sentences which imply that the sentence with the opposite meaning has been definitively cut off! It is this definitive cutting-off that procures this particular jouissance, the jouissance of the reputedly noble activity that is called thinking. This is exactly what happens with Plato – I think it is in *The Sophist* – with the definition of the angler: if you want to arrive at the concept, you have to keep cutting off, cutting off, cutting off, cutting off. What jouissance! Because it is a cutting-off which is carried out not in the name of a father but in the name of what you will end up calling reason.

Z, W, 3.80, WLK. 3.80? Look, there's something in that – you're going to say, Melman's going off the rails – 3.80 is not the interior eight, it's the eight cut down the middle vertically: the 3! It's absurd, it's crazy, how can you say such a thing? Well, let's say something else, let's say that all these letters that mark the life of the obsessional ... I say that the life of the obsessional unfolds between *eins, zwei, drei* – one, two, three, but you have to say it in German! The rest doesn't count, the little brothers and the little sisters can't possibly count, because he stops at 3.

And with the Z, the W, the L, the K you have a thing that I'm quite sure has astonished you: these letters are all made through the dispositions of a unary trait combined in various ways. How, with the One, can we manage to make something of the letter using a combination of these traits? I expect you'll say again, he's kidding, what's he going on about, who's going to prove that to me? But Chinese script consists of nothing else! It comprises unary traits which are varied, diverse, aesthetic arrangements and constitute the letter. This passage, the constitution of the writing of the letter based on the unary trait, is the victory of the obsessional. From this moment on there is, theoretically, no longer any hiatus. The great problem is the union of the One and the letter, the One and the small *a*, which are fundamentally discordant. But if the letter is constituted from the One itself, isn't that the most beautiful victory, the most beautiful success? It means you will now be able to count in rats, since the rat becomes a unit from now on, a monetary unit, a One among others! Obviously, we are now right in the midst of an obsessional fantasy.

This Rosetta Stone is thus a striking illustration of the ways in which we are victims of the signifier, because I can assure you that is not the obsessional's fault. As in the case of the little girl I was talking about a while back, who had become obsessional because her little brother was dead – obviously with the implication that she had wished it to be so – well, it wasn't her fault, either! Where the fault lies is in our dependency on the signifier, both in our cogitations and in our social life.

The true neurosis – why the true one? Because it is determined entirely by fixation, by the relation to the Other, which at the same time isolates us from our neighbour because we have nothing but a death wish as far as he is concerned. Obsessional neurosis does not make bonds. It makes everybody find jouissance in his own corner using his own product, in fantasies of equality, justice, and accountability. Why, indeed, does the obsessional have to count rapidly between the lightning and the thunderclap, if not to fill this space, which is supposedly empty, with ... numbers, so that it will be a totality, completely compact. We can observe that our relation to money, which dominates social life far more than sex does, is entirely regulated by a set-up of the obsessional type. Hysteria is based on a discourse; in perversion, the relation to others is paramount; and in phobia, there is always the need for another person to accompany you.

A very long time ago, I happened to have a patient whose symptom was that she found it difficult to go out, because she had to locate all the places along the way, usually Bistros, where she could use the toilet if she needed to. Maybe some of you have had similar cases. The fear of not being able to find a suitable place for evacuation is eminently obsessional – whether it is blocked, closed, sewn up – look, we talk about sewing up people's lips, but no-one has ever thought of another torture that would involve sewing up something else ... the thought that this natural object would not be able to ... well, it caused her significant torments. Otherwise, her thinking was completely intact and integral.

There is only one route which, contrary to the usual ways, does not situate its object in the field of representations; only one, and it is the way of those theologians who keep striving, who live in a state of suffering: will we manage to stitch up, to patch up the space that separates us? In this case we are referring to gnosticism. But are we to remain caught up in what is essentially a negative theology? Whatever one may say about this god, it's never that! These theologians are the only ones! Have a look at Gilson's *The Spirit of Mediaeval Philosophy*, you are in for a treat. I have to say that reading this little book disturbs me, it's so delicious to be going round and round this missing object, unless you are dealing with theologians in a virtual infinity; and at that very moment you are back in the midst of consecrated, common obsessional neurosis, even if as St Thomas and Lacan remind us, at the end of all that – and did Lacan say it about the end of analysis as well? – *sicut palea*, which you could translate in a rather unhygienic way: "It was all just a load of shit!"

I do not mean to finish on a pessimistic note, but rather to say that being a pile of rags is just part of the human condition. Oh, you didn't realise we are just a pile of rags? We are rags [*loques*] because we are at a conference [*colloque*] – a *col-loque*, which gathers all the rags together. "But of course", you will reply: "speakers [*locuteurs*], *loques-uteurs*, who know that everything they say is full of holes". And what is more, they repeat it: "What one says remains forgotten behind what is understood"; so if I give a nice paper, I shall try to make you forget that it is never anything more than something spoken, which comes out of a hole. And if you are scientific and not religious, whatever is found in this hole to animate my talk will not be the divine One, but the object *a*, because it is either the one or the other.

The obsessional carries out this work of stitching, in order to patch up this rag that we are talking about today; he works away to stitch the rag back together; and I think we should come dressed in cast-off clothes ... maybe monks' cowls. But I would feel I hadn't gone all the way, if I hadn't proposed a complete decoding of Freud's case, page by page. It seems to me that its subversive nature is a virtual possibility, so that we should not always, in our own work, be caught up in this seam-stresses' work, stitching, repairing – it is work which can only ever be a waste of time; and so that we should get far better results from the laws of language, rather than trying to heal ourselves, or obtain jouissance, or repair.

Notes

1. Conference paper given by Charles Melman (Association lacanienne internationale) on 13th March 2016.
2. Melman gave a seminar on Freud's Rat Man case over a period of two years, from 1987 to 1989; Melman, 2015. [Ed.]
3. The concept of oblativity is expanded on by Bosetti in chapter four of this book. [Ed.]

References

Gilson, E. (1922). *La philosophie au moyen-âge.* Paris: Payot, 1988.
Melman, C. (2015). *La névrose obsessionelle.* Toulouse: Érès.

CHAPTER SEVEN

The Lacanian structure of obsessional neurosis[1]

MICHEL SILVESTRE

Preface by Danièle Silvestre

I cannot give a precise date when this paper was written. I know only that it was presented orally at Caracas in Venezuela at the beginning of the 1980s, probably in 1982. It was for a seminar of the Freudian field, organised by Diana Rabinovitch, who had invited Michel to speak about obsessional neurosis. So, he wrote a paper for oral presentation, and this means that a certain amount of reworking has been necessary, in order to make it suitable for publication. To be honest, I did not want to risk altering his style, so there may be repetitions and moments of tedium – too bad! The development of the ideas is extremely rigorous, which makes it easier to read.

When Nancy Katan-Barwell, on behalf of the editorial committee of the Revue Nationale des Collèges Cliniques Champ Freudien asked me to find a clinical paper from the archives of Michel Silvestre for the Journal, I was not sure I would be able to do so. However, this paper seemed to me to be appropriate and really useful. Although it is more than twenty years old [at the time of the French publication], it still remains relevant today, and his style, which I have taken great care to preserve, is modern. There were in fact three presentations on the subject, which correspond to the three sections of the paper; it would have been a pity to cut it up for publication (publishing it across more than one issue of the journal), and even more of a pity to abridge it. So here it is in its entirety, a work-in-progress, unfinished, but at the same time of value because of the opening it offers for reflection, and because of the trains of thought that it follows. I am happy to recommend it to the reader, and would like to thank Nancy for initiating its publication.

Danièle Silvestre

The Lacanian structure of obsessional neurosis

When Diana Rabinovitch asked me to come here this year to speak with you about obsessional neurosis, the prospect of the journey and of spending time here filled me with joy rather more than the theme itself, which might have made me hesitate to come. What is there to say that might be a bit new, on a theme that is so very old?

What is more, I had been told categorically that you were all broadly familiar with Freud and the Rat Man case, and that what was required was something Lacanian and to the point. So, what I thought I would try to tell you is something based on the work that we have been doing in Paris, particularly in the Section Clinique, since our fundamental aim is to set up a working community, which means communicating about a certain number of psychoanalytic ideas based on the teaching of Lacan. And so, the title I am proposing to you may now perhaps seem somewhat more reasonable.

Obsessional neurosis is an old refrain of psychoanalysis. It doesn't have the reputation of brilliance, of inventiveness, of surprise, that hysterical neurosis has. But that is obsessional neurosis as we, analysts, think we know it. What I am referring to is obsessional neurosis in psychoanalysis, because I hardly need to remind you that the psychiatric tradition is quite different.

The obsessional, according to the psychiatric tradition, is a very turbulent individual, anxious, agitated by his anxiety, and his impulsive behaviour has always been emphasised: from suicide to murder, via fugue states, disappearances, bankruptcies, indeed all the intemperate behaviours which never cease to disturb psychiatrists. And, at heart, the Rat Man (yes, I shall speak about him a little, after all) is indeed a rather picturesque individual.

So, the task is to explain how and why the obsessional has moved from being this highly colourful figure, who has no reason to envy the hysteric, to being a caricature of the living dead, the professional inhibited person, which is the view peddled in the analytic literature. How is it that this hugely anxious person, who is always a hair's breadth away from leaping at the throat of his neighbour or ruining his family with the first hysteric who comes along, this terribly "nervous" person who is constantly troubled, can be transformed into a character we can only describe as a "dear old grandpa", just by dint of lying down on a couch?

Dear old grandpa is a term with explicitly paternal connotations, and it will be one of the axes of my talk. My first observation is that the obsessional finds paternal support in the analytic treatment that will enable him to block out his anxiety, but the price he pays will be a reinforcement of his neurosis. So, what is required is to alter the angle from which the question is approached so that we can encourage the emergence of a new obsessional. Well, this new obsessional will not be found by reorganising symptoms or structure, but rather in the consequences that this reorganisation will have on our practice.

In other words, it is a question of re-actualising, reactivating the obsessional neurosis, and on that basis, we can find some pointers as to how we should conduct the treatment.

The structural clinic of obsessional neurosis

If structure is of any use at all, it has to be because it implies a constraint within which the analyst's own practice is caught up. To put it another way, it is not only a question of orientating the symptomatology, that is to say of discriminating in the field of semiology (which is still barely separated from psychiatry) between whatever effectively belongs to obsessional neurosis and to the analytic symptom, since the symptom is equivalent to the structure, and what is merely an epiphenomenon. But it is even more important to find the proper axis to orientate our practice.

It is worth pointing out that if we can be authorised to make a conjunction between clinic and structure, it is because structure in the Lacanian sense is something quite specific. It is a supple structure, and we can say it is full of emptiness, since it rests on two principles:

1) The subject is only ever represented by a signifier and moreover, for another signifier, which itself is always other. In other words,

the subject is never anything but the gap between two signifiers, that is to say, a nothing, but precisely a nothing without which the signifying structure would be unthinkable.

2)   That the signifier infallibly misses the real – put another way, you can never obtain jouissance from the thing – and this failure is what produces the object *a*, which is precisely that to which the subject's access to jouissance is reduced.

Fundamentally, if we wished to systematise and obsessionalise our clinic of obsessional neurosis, we could try to divide up symptomatology according to these two aspects of lack in the structure:

*   on the side of lack of the signifier, we could place obsession, ritual, doubt;
*   on the side of lack of the object, we could place ambivalence and aggressivity.

That does not seem very convincing to me, because if we used this approach, we would be obeying the major obsessional trait: the ruse according to which the obsessional is always somewhere other than in the place where you are trying to catch him. His aim is to escape being caught by anything, whether a signifier or an object. He is someone whose response is always to say he is "absent", because the only place from which he could not avoid responding would be from the place of anxiety; but it is from there, obviously, that it is impossible for him to reply, because in the place of anxiety, he as a subject vanishes.

These propositions, obvious everyday phenomena of obsessional neurosis, have to be justified structurally. That is why it seemed to me to be necessary to find a fixed point from which, possibly, I might be able to reel off and justify the series of symptoms of obsessional neurosis. And, according to Lacan, there is no fixed point without a fiction which itself is capable of producing truth; we shall see if we find this approach convincing. So, let us hold on to this notion of fiction; but it is not just any old fiction, since it is one that is central to psychoanalytic theory, and stems originally from Freud.

So here it is: obsessional neurosis is constituted in relation to a very particular Other, centred on the anal object. Of course, this is a psychoanalytic trick, but certainly not one to disdain, since Lacan illustrates it precisely in the clinic of this object, in his seminar on anxiety. Of course, it is not a question of transposing Abraham's stages into Lacanian terms, nor of matching with each of the various forms of the Lacanian object *a* (breast, faeces, gaze, voice) a neurosis that would be directly linked with it. It is probable that for any subject, each of these objects organises his relation to the world, in successive moments of his fantasy.

Nonetheless, it is clear that for any given subject, this relation to the world, which is to say, to the Other, reveals a prevalence, which casts its shadow, and colours other objects; this is what Freud called the fusion of the drives. One of the functions of analysis is certainly to untangle this fusion, and to bring the prevalence to light, so that, in the best of outcomes, the fundamental fantasy can be revealed. This is what we can see at work in the obsessional: his entire relation to the world implies a transposition of his relation to the anal object. And what is particular about the anal object, if not that it is central to the Other's demand, the demand addressed by the Other to the subject; the oral object is also linked to the Other's demand, but more in the form of an appeal to (towards) the Other.

But we have to be clear that the object is not the effect of desire, it is the cause of it. And the anal object as cause has the particular feature that it is only the cause of desire in so far as it is retained, held on to by the subject, in other words, refused to the Other who demands it; fundamentally, that is what the fiction-fixation is.

So, we see that desire, as soon as it has fixed on this object, puts the subject into a very special situation: either he submits to the demand of the Other, and his desire is extinguished, or the subject attains his desire, and has to be able to bear to refuse himself to the Other, to disobey him, in other words, to lose his love. Put another way, the anal object introduces the subject to an antinomy between what would be his own desire, and what comes to him as a demand from the Other. That is true for all subjects, in so far as they cannot avoid having to deal with the anal object. So, the subject who "chooses" to become obsessional is the one who relies on the demand of the Other to distance himself from his own desire, or rather, according to Lacan, to emphasise the impossibility of it.

Freud gives a very nice illustration of this relation of the obsessional to the demand of the Other, in a short paper entitled, "The disposition to obsessional neurosis" (1913i). He shows that this neurosis is triggered when the Other, embodied in this case by the sexual partner, demands that the subject becomes desiring. When the subject has to specify what his desire is, he recoils in the face of this request, and an obsessional neurosis is triggered. Clearly, the obsessional does not escape suffering where this repudiation of desire is concerned. Let us look further into the consequences of this fiction. Clinging to the demand of the Other has another implication, namely that it also means a negation of the desire of the Other; because if the Other is present only in the form of the one who makes demands, this implies that if he gets what he demands, he can satisfy himself with it. In other words, the Other who demands is not the Other who desires.

The Other who desires lacks something, and the subject does not have the power to supply what is lacking. This is why the emergence of the desire of the Other generates anxiety, and that is the last thing the obsessional wants. From this comes his defence against anxiety which he promotes in the form of fantasy; but it is a fantasy whose object responds to, and constructs itself around, the demand of the Other.

So, while the hysteric maintains desire, even at the price of anxiety, the obsessional protects himself from anxiety at the price of a fantasy which he constructs at the whim of the Other. What terrifies the obsessional the most is the prospect of being confronted with desire, in so far as it is the desire of the Other, by which we mean in so far as it introduces the dimension of the Other as sexuated. The passage from the demand of the Other to the desire of the Other implies the introduction of sexual difference, in other words, of sexual jouissance. In this regard, the obsessional is fundamentally sexually obsessed. It is via sexual jouissance that his desire is structured; but it is structured around rejection, misapprehension, refusal, and the passion to know nothing of this jouissance.

Desire, in so far as it is caused by a lack, is sustained by a double impasse; for obviously in order for desire to be preserved, the lack must persist. It can be preserved in one of two ways: either by maintaining any given object as unsatisfactory (this is the hysteric's solution) or by maintaining jouissance – in this case, the aim of desire – as impossible (which is the obsessional's solution).

What we need to grasp is that when Lacan says that the obsessional's desire is an impossible desire, we have to understand that it is because this desire presents itself as impossible that the obsessional can continue to desire. For the obsessional, impossibility is what safeguards desire. But one rather dramatic consequence of this is that maintaining desire as impossible can only reinforce the superego's injunction to obtain jouissance. This helps us to put into perspective the whole gamut of symptoms that arise from obsession in the strict sense of the word. The *Zwang*, along with the obsessions and rituals that are responses to it, are the avatars of the desperate return to a jouissance that is irremediably lost and yet nonetheless never ceases to be invoked.

This superegoic injunction is precisely the demand of the Other who puts it into words. We could even say that the obsessional obtains jouissance from refusing the demand of the Other. But it is a jouissance that terrorises him, and he wants to know nothing of it; he refutes it absolutely. He refutes it because it interrogates the Other directly, without mediation via the pacifying channel of the Name-of-the-Father. This is why the obsessional is willingly disappointed by phallic jouissance, but at the same time he clings to it desperately, because it affords him protection from the oedipal field. The obsessional is obsessed by jouissance.

So, we have made some progress, because we have now established the following:

1) The obsessional attaches himself to the demand of the Other in order to obliterate desire.
2) In the face of this demand, he cannot maintain his desire unless he endows it with the exclusive aim of jouissance.
3) But this aim of jouissance, this obsession with jouissance, implies that his desire is marked by an impossibility.

Having established this much, we can highlight three obsessional traits: the organisation of the fantasy, the mode of emergence of anxiety, and the frequency of acting-out. We may posit here, as a deduction, that his fantasy is a response to the demand of the Other, and this response has the function of:

1) preserving the subject's desire, and
2) protecting the subject, at the same time, from the desire of the Other.

This points to one thing: that the object of the fantasy will be the one which the subject supposes the Other demands of him. In the fantasy, what is demanded by the Other will assume the function of the object, and the subject has no choice but to identify with this object, because he cannot give this object, he cannot detach himself from it, unless he renounces his own desire. This is what Lacan proposes in his paper "Subversion of the subject and the dialectic of desire" (Lacan, 1966, pp. 671–702), observing that the obsessional can only maintain his desire by accentuating its impossibility – meaning: the jouissance of the Other – through the fading of the subject; he identifies with the object of his fantasy in order to annihilate himself as subject. This allows us to explain other obsessional traits such as depersonalisation.

This is where we situate all the obsessional's ambiguities where gifts are concerned. It is not that he is a giver of gifts, or conversely that he rebels against such giving; it is that the only gift he can give is himself. And that is how he loves, too. While to love is to give what one does not have, we can see that what the obsessional puts on the scales of love is his very life, his existence. That is why, contrary to all appearances, the obsessional, in spite of all his efforts, is a lover, or more precisely, a man of passion; but only on condition that he keeps it quiet.

The obsessional is a man of passion who stirs up passions in order to misapprehend them. As soon as he is in a position to speak about them, they disappear, because speaking of them would lift the veil from the desire of the Other, and would throw him into a state of anxiety. Indeed, he is doomed to become anxious from the moment when he becomes engaged in the demand which he addresses to the Other, as soon as he speaks to the Other, and a place is cleared where desire could emerge. From that moment on, the fiction that the Other is pure demand fractures, and the obsessional becomes prey to anxiety. This is why he makes a habit of acting out, since this allows him to stir up his own desire so that the Other can be the silent witness of it, while he, the obsessional, can remain in a state of misapprehension regarding his desire – a misapprehension which may take on the appearance of a withdrawal, or even of indifference.

These latter points assume all their importance in the way we direct the treatment. But, in order to bring this presentation of the clinic of obsessional neurosis to a conclusion, I would like to explore an aspect of it which is important because it relates specifically to the obsessional's propensity to place difficulties in the way of the treatment itself. It relates to the preponderance of the imaginary register in obsessional neurosis. You might think that Lacanian theory, since it has established a notion of the structure of the subject, would allow us to "neglect" the imaginary. In my view, this would be a mistake. We have recourse to the symbolic precisely in order to "treat" the imaginary, and if possible to bring about changes in it. Furthermore, it is one aspect of the logic of the fantasy that it helps to expose the way in which the subject's imaginary is organised, and thus allows the analyst to find a pathway through it.

On the other hand, we should not lose sight of the fact that while the analyst works with the signifier (i.e., in the symbolic), the effects of his acts become manifest at the level of the imaginary, the whole question being whether these effects will be durable and, if that is the case, if the subjective structure has been shaken up.

Lacan himself emphasised that one of the aims of analysis consists in re-modelling the identifications. From the 1960s onwards, he began to envisage something beyond this aim – at the same time as the object of the fantasy was progressively acquiring the status of real object and no longer of a merely imaginary one. It seems to me that one of the most solid axes from which to approach this question is to bear in mind that the ego is not the subject, and even, especially for the obsessional, that the ego is an object – an imaginary object – for the subject, in the same way as is the little other. This is essential, because precisely on this point, the hysteric makes things easy for us. For the hysteric, the ego is confused with a little other, certainly a privileged one, but one that can immediately be identified as such. This means that the position of the hysteric can quite easily be located thanks to her enunciations. The subject is separated from the envelope of the ego. It is divided by the signifier.

This is one of the reasons why there is a discourse of the hysteric, because the hysteric pushes the subject – the subject of the unconscious – into the foreground. The hysteric dresses up, disguises herself, with the semblance of the divided subject. Her speech is instated into the discourse without further ado.

Where the obsessional is concerned, it is different. He sends his ego onto the battlefield. The obsessional subject is fundamentally a "shirker"; obviously that does not stop him from suffering; on the contrary, it makes him suffer. The more he shirks as a subject, the more his ego has to take it straight on the chin. His ego – or rather, his other; it really does not matter to him, because after all, they are equivalent. This even constitutes the well-spring of the obsessional's renowned aggressivity, the extraordinary facility he has for getting embroiled in imaginary confrontations, his delight in them, from which analysis has the greatest difficulty in extricating him.

We may say that the obsessional, like the hysteric, speaks with the other; but the hysteric speaks whether or not her ego is included in the other, while the obsessional speaks with his ego as if it were the other, but in the way I would speak using a microphone. This imaginary equivalence between the ego and the other – i(a) – illuminates an essential trait (the last one on my list, I think), which we call ambivalence. Ambivalence is ultimately, at the level of the passions, the mode of expression of the division of the obsessional subject. The obsessional, more than the hysteric, is the dupe of his imaginary. He is primarily divided by his passions, by his affects, which are taken on board by his objects, the ego and the other, the ego and its double. The subject himself, as Lacan has shown, is in the room, so he is present at the confrontation and can count the blows.

This is why he needs a rule of arbitration. Or rather, he supposes necessarily and desperately that such a rule exists. In other words, his withdrawal from the scene implies the existence of an Other who ensures that this rule is applied. The participants need a safety net. The obsessional is fundamentally a believer (cf. his relation to the father and to religion). This is what Lacan meant when he said that the obsessional stands surety for the Other. And this surety, it seems to me, can be seen as a new avatar of that which he believes the Other is demanding from him.

The obsessional's entry into analysis

I thought that in order to bring us closer to the more clinical aspects, i.e., case studies, we should take some time to explore the question of the entry into analysis, and obviously, given the direction I am taking us in, I will link this with the triggering of neurosis.

Indeed, while we speak generally of the triggering of psychosis, the question of the triggering of neurosis seems to be left aside. More precisely, it seems that the neurosis has always been there, and for the subject its emergence is neither noted nor noticed. Obviously, there is a reason for that: the Freudian conception of psychical reality. And that concerns the distinction between the real and reality. In fact, it is from the moment when we can distinguish the dimension of the real that we can justify the following:

1) Life is not a dream,
2) it is possible to wake up,

3) and you don't necessarily fall asleep again exactly the same as you
    were before.

In fact, if we just take the relation between the imaginary and the
symbolic, there is nothing to stop us supposing that there is a sort of
balance – which may be neurotic, but the elements of it are all there,
given in their entirety in a sort of atemporality. It is precisely this conception that implies that there is a genesis, which occurs when this balance is created. Inversely, as soon as you introduce the dimension of the
real alongside the other two, you have to admit that psychical reality is
rather precarious, as is the balance between imaginary and symbolic;
and in this way, you may neglect to include this genetic dimension,
since the advent of the subject is situated in a relation between psychical reality and encounter, and not between psychical reality and maturation of the drives.

So, if we take the real into consideration, we are necessarily led to
ask ourselves the question about a triggering, that is to say, about the
encounter with an element of the real, something which imperils psychical reality and brings about a psychical restructuring. I think we
should always bear in mind that it is this context into which we, as analysts, are asked to introduce ourselves when a demand for analysis is
addressed to us. We come in some way to complement a psychical state
that has become destabilised, and fundamentally we come to position
ourselves in this very place where the event has triggered something
overwhelming for the subject.

This explains why Lacan, in the final phase of his teaching and his
practice, could make of the encounter with the analyst – i.e., of the session – an encounter with the real. The important thing being that the
transference should allow and support a manoeuvre, a strategy, in these
encounters. Why? Because the agent of the encounter – nothing other
than jouissance – will clothe itself in the semblance.

So, there is a triggering of neurosis just as there are conditions for
entry into analysis. Obviously, it is because there are conditions for
entry into analysis that we can, on that basis and retroactively, locate
the triggering. The entry into analysis is evidence of such triggering,
but more so with the obsessional than with the hysteric, because obsessional neurosis, more than hysteria, is a neurosis that can be designated
as intrasubjective. Once again, it is important to distinguish clearly
between what emanates from the ego and what from the subject.

As soon as the obsessional delegates the gamut of his difficulties, his perplexities, and his inhibitions, to his ego, he can continue to live in ignorance, even in the most perfect serenity. It is his ego which shoulders the burdens of the world, not he himself. He may live a very long time with his symptoms (obsession, rituals, actings-out) without having the faintest perception of their existence; he, the obsessional, is not inside this obsessional world. And we realise straight away what this implies concerning his entry into analysis. The latter may have two completely opposing consequences. Either he may find a new equilibrium, because in analysis he has found the support that he had been missing (and we shall see what sort of support is meant here), or else the analyst refuses to act merely as a support, and the activation of the treatment tends rather to accentuate the instability, with the risk that the subject will immediately flee from analysis.

But first, I would like to illustrate these questions with reference to our most famous obsessional: the Rat Man. I do not think it completely useless to return to this case, because when we revisited it in our clinical section, we found that we were far from having exhausted its treasures, and in particular, where the Rat Man's entry into analysis is concerned. His entry into analysis was marked by three moments, which I shall enumerate in this way: the awakening, the ineffectiveness of the symptom, and the constitution of the subject-supposed-to-know.

The awakening was obviously the encounter with the cruel captain, or rather, the moment when the latter described the famous torture to the Rat Man. And what happened? The Rat Man was overcome with anxiety and went mad. There was something in this story that he could not bear, which Freud linked unambiguously to a certain jouissance. A jouissance, he would point out, "he wanted to know nothing about".

So, the first moment: jouissance and overwhelming anxiety which split apart and breached the little obsessional world of the young man, and upset his homoeostasis.

The second moment: the symptom that did not work. Through the breach caused by the awakening, let us say the breach of jouissance, the *Zwang* (compulsion) was introduced: you must pay back the money; and the obsession: the extraordinary scenario according to which he had to repay the money, which was of an almost delusional complexity, but where nevertheless the absurd justification for each action attests to its value as a ritual. And by the way, you will notice that this scenario produces a veritable multiplication of little others, each of whom has their prescribed role. The failure of this symptom – I'm going to tell you what I mean by failure – is obviously that no gaps are filled; there is no chance for the Rat Man to return to his tranquil world. His scenario is impossible, because from the very beginning, he does not owe anything. It is rather a question of another debt, a symbolic one: his own father's debt, which he will only be able to pay off through engaging in analysis. So, the symptom fails, and anxiety persists.

The third moment: the constitution of the subject-supposed-to-know. The Rat Man finds one of Freud's books at the home of his friend Gutman, in which he sees that there is at least one person – Freud – who can understand what is happening to him, and who gives the impression of being able to do something about it, for example, creating knowledge out if it. He goes to see Freud, and fundamentally, very quickly, right from the first session – which Freud himself qualifies as a preliminary one – his symptom finds someone to address itself to. In other words, Freud found a perfectly fitting place from which to constitute an analytic couple with the Rat Man. The Rat Man's disorder, his intrasubjective instability, could thus become an intersubjective disorder. We may say that there were now two of them who could become involved in this disorder.

Well, fundamentally, making an extreme simplification, we may say that the Rat Man's entry into neurosis was the passage from moment 1 to moment 2, or if you prefer, from anxiety to the symptom; from anxiety that resulted from a jouissance that could not be controlled, to a symptom that tried but failed to exercise control. And the entry into analysis was the passage from this inadequate symptom to the discovery of a locus where speech could be addressed, in other words, the constitution of the subject-supposed-to-know.

I am going to leave the Rat Man now, and just hold on to the schema the case has enabled us to construct. On the basis of this I am going to lay down some structural markers for the obsessional's entry into analysis. The triggering of the neurosis springs from a *"tuché"*, an encounter with the real. According to Lacan, the way the real manifests itself is through the forms in which object *a* appears. In my view, there are three – at least where neurosis is concerned – which seem to correspond to the three types of neurosis: jouissance, anxiety, and conversion, by which I mean the body when it is awakened into a state of aberrant jouissance or suffering. The latter is basically what the hysteric displays when her body has become deranged through the workings of conversion. Anxiety obviously refers to phobic neurosis; in this case, the situation that generates the phobia becomes real, breaking out from psychical reality. For the obsessional, it is the irruption of a certain jouissance that throws the fantasy off-balance.

So, let us focus on the obsessional: he is particularly preoccupied with jouissance, but what preoccupies him above all is to maintain this jouissance under the ferrule of the phallus. In other words, he struggles to maintain this jouissance in the order of accounting, of finitude. The fact that this leads him to keep on counting, to regret that this jouissance is limited, is preferable for him to an unlimited jouissance. Where the obsessional loses his bearings is the point at which something enters his field that threatens him with an unlimited jouissance, or at least its possibility, a jouissance of "not-all" – what Lacan calls the jouissance of the Other.

This explains two things:

1) that obsessional neurosis is the most common form of neurosis in men, because the penis (and the way it functions) imposes on them the imagination of a jouissance that is limited and can be counted (stroke by stroke);

2) that the obsessional man is habitually so preoccupied with his partner's jouissance, that he either becomes obsessed with it (which leads to the symptoms of premature ejaculation or impotence), or the opposite – he does not want to know anything about it, and denies it absolutely. But that is not sufficient to trigger a neurosis; something else is needed, namely that it should be supported, introduced by a demand. If this demand is explicitly a demand to obtain jouissance, the obsessional "cracks up", he throws in the sponge, because he has been forced to enter the unbounded zone of the jouissance of the Other.

In this demand for jouissance you can recognise the fundamental, primordial superegoic injunction. Jouissance is one of the burdens, perhaps the heaviest, that weighs on the shoulders of the speaking being. Jouissance is that "whose absence would render the universe vain" (Lacan, 1966, p. 694). You can see that running the risk of causing the universe to be vain through lack of jouissance is a big responsibility, and is the source of the sense of guilt. Fortunately, the Oedipus complex allows the subject to organise some sort of pact with jouissance:

there is castration, thanks to which a certain way of engaging with jouissance is possible; and this engagement is regulated via the law of the father through phallic signification. It is the Name-of-the-Father which ordains that the subject may have access to jouissance, at the price of castration. The only thing is, this pact leaves out the jouissance of the Other. And what connects the jouissance of the Other with the subject is the superego, the injunction to engage with jouissance which is unregulated, wild, extra-phallic, i.e., outside of castration.

The obsessional clings to this phallic jouissance because in it he refinds himself, and he imagines that he can control it. The only thing is, he refuses to pay the price (by offering the gift of his castration to the other), or at least he quibbles, he haggles. Also, the more he hangs on to phallic jouissance, the more he is threatened by the jouissance of the Other, because they can only be apportioned if castration is recognised. This is why the obsessional reinforces the father in the imaginary register, so that he can find support in it, to protect himself from this threat. This is why he appears to be so touchy, so apt to form a severe superego, which then, indeed, summons him towards this jouissance of the Other.

We can see this superego incarnated for the Rat Man in the obscene and ferocious figure of the cruel captain. But I also think that you will find some sort of equivalent in most obsessionals at the moment when their neurosis becomes manifest. Sometimes it will be a woman, legitimate or otherwise, who demands that the subject get out of his more or less masturbatory rut; or it may be a double, the subject's ego ideal which renounces the role of being the sole support of the jouissance of the Other. Sometimes it will be an event in the subject's professional life – a promotion, or the opposite, a failure – which will force the subject to face his unravelling when confronted with this injunction.

So that is how it works when the obsessional is awakened by the encounter with the real of jouissance.

The constitution, or even the accentuation of the symptom, is the second moment. The symptom, like the Name-of-the-Father, is one of the supports of phallic jouissance. The symptom, indeed, is the response with which the subject mitigates the absence of the sexual relation, in other words, the real of sex. In this way, we may understand that the symptom in itself constitutes a form of satisfaction, of jouissance. When the obsessional loses his footing in the face of the superego's injunction to jouissance, everything that supports phallic jouissance will be reinforced, with a greater or lesser degree of success. This often fails, because such is his attachment to the demand of the Other that it is very difficult for him to silence it once it has taken on the countenance of the superego. This failure usually involves an even greater intensification of the symptom.

The other option, which is the one the Rat Man chose, is to make an appeal to the father. It is a father whom he imagines to be capable of controlling this deregulated jouissance and bringing it within the bounds of reason. This is why the obsessional's imaginary figurine of the father is always ambiguous, because at one moment it incarnates the Other, pacified by the law, the one who reigns over desire and ordains jouissance – the oedipal father; but behind this image, we can usually see what we can call Father jouissance, the one constructed by Freud in *Totem and Taboo* (Freud, 1912–1913), the one who obtains unrestricted jouissance and cares nothing about castration. We can observe that in the family constellation of the obsessional, this position of jouissance is in fact occupied by the mother. But it takes a certain amount of time to move on from the obsessional's beginnings in analysis, before he can realise this.

So, you can see the sorts of auspices under which the obsessional may find his way into analysis: establishing that the symptom is only making his suffering worse will lead him inevitably to seek a father; a father who appears as guarantor of his jouissance while pacifying his access to it. Freud shows a deep understanding of this since he directs the whole of the treatment towards this father, and it becomes a question of paying off the father's debt. And yet looking for a father does not explain why you find an analyst. What remains to be explained is the transference (in the sense of a displacement) from the cruel captain to Freud; in one of the early sessions, the Rat Man calls Freud "my Captain".

How is the transference put in place for the obsessional, or how is the subject-supposed-to-know instituted; or, putting it another way, how does the obsessional enter into the analytic discourse? There is only one clinical category to which Lacan attributed a discourse: hysteria. As for the others, we need to find out which door they use to enter this little world.

There is at least one discourse that is suitable for any speaking being (apart from the psychotic): the discourse of the master. It is fundamentally the equivalent of the discourse of the unconscious, as illustrated in particular by the obsessional (for example the signifier *Zwang* is equivalent to a master signifier). But in its primitive form it is not a social bond. In order for the other, the analyst, to be included in this discourse, we need the pathway via the subject-supposed-to-know, in other words the introduction of a third term in relation to the analytic couple, in the form of a signifier alongside which the subject can be represented.

Let us return to our Freudian example, the Rat Man. He goes to see Freud, and what does he bring him? A signifier that represents him perfectly; indeed, so well that Freud uses it to name him: rat. Rat, which is what Lacan calls the signifier of the transference. The social bond can be created when the signifier of the subject-supposed-to-know comes into the place of Sq as a second signifier that represents the subject. So, what is it that marks Freud in the eyes of the Rat Man? Of course, by what is clearly accentuated: that he knows what his symptom is referring to, what jouissance is included in his symptom. In other words, Freud incarnates the subject-supposed-to-know about jouissance, which we can write as S/a; thus, the algorithm of the transference makes way for the matheme of the discourse of the master (see Lacan, 1995, pp. 4f).

The discourse of the master is the privileged discourse through which the obsessional can make a bond with the analyst. Now, here you may suspect that there will be an obvious difficulty: the discourse of the master is not the analytic discourse; the elements are there, but not in their right place. In fact, as we have seen, the obsessional will find an analyst in order to go back to sleep, to return to his subjective non-existence, so he seeks nothing more than a kind master who will watch over his slumbers. There is an equally strong temptation for the analyst to take up this position of mastery, and to orientate his interpretations in the direction of an injunction that will banish everything but the ego from the analysis. Clearly, awareness of this is essential for the direction of the treatment.

What remains now is to show how, as soon as the obsessional invites the analyst to occupy the place of the master, the analyst can succeed in drawing him into the discourse of the analyst. How, as soon as the obsessional addresses this demand to the analyst: "Shut this jouissance up, I don't want to know anything about it!" the analyst can reply to him: "It is the knowledge about this jouissance that constitutes your truth!"

In other words, the analyst has to bring out this response: "This jouissance is a semblance, it is only of interest to you in as much as your truth supports it" (a/S2). It cannot be denied that there is a rift in this about-turn – as Lacan says, the discourse of the master is the "other side" of analysis – and this rift is all the more striking when you make an equivalence between the discourse of the master and the discourse of the unconscious. The latter is not made to be analysed; it is self-sufficient. According to Lacan, it is the ideal worker, based on the impossible mastery of what it knows. We may well ask how analysis could possibly have been invented, since the unconscious shows itself to be so stubborn. But then we are forgetting the hysteric, and indeed, what allows the obsessional to turn towards analysis is what Lacan calls hystericisation.

This means that suffering is solicited, the subject is solicited to uphold his complaint and to allow his division to emerge, at the risk of increasing it. The hysteric insists that this suffering spouts out of the body. That is what is particular about hysteria.

The obsessional does not suffer with his body, although it could happen to him. No, usually he suffers from what is demanded of him. To put it simply, he suffers from everything that is said to him by others; for he sees a demand hidden in every word addressed to him. The only thing is, if the obsessional is hystericised, he does not become a hysteric as such. Because while this demand is behind his complaint, do not forget that it is also the source of the jouissance he does not want to know anything about. So, his complaint about the demand of the Other is ambiguous.

What is at stake in this complaint is basically the terrorising attraction to the jouissance of the Other. This is why he will continue to build a bulwark around himself in the form of phallic jouissance. This in turn means that this complaint, this suffering which enables him to become hystericised, will be supported by his impotence, his castration – which means he can be reassured regarding the limits of his jouissance.

The obsessional makes much of his castration so it can be the alibi for everything he has renounced. This is why he clings on to it. "Don't demand anything of me, you can see how weak I am." This signifies that the castration in question is only ever an imaginary castration. What he manages to preserve by exalting it in this way (it is a lure, a diversionary manoeuvre) is the castration of the Other, in other words, the Other's desire. So, the obsessional's suffering is difficult to evaluate; if indeed it is a sign of his hystercisation, then it corresponds to the prevalence of the imaginary we find in obsessionals. This is why we still have work to do.

Direction of the treatment in obsessional neurosis

So – we left our obsessional at the moment of entry into analysis.

We can be sure of one thing: all of his unhappiness is rooted in his relation to jouissance. He is unhappy, but that is also his only reason for living. The obsessional, to paraphrase Freud, lives in a constant state of nostalgia for his lost jouissance.

We should not jump too quickly to the conclusion that this nostalgia is equivalent to the bond with the mother. If the obsessional, especially in the case of a man, appears to be desperately attached to his mother, it is equally because it is she who sets off the imaginary father to advantage. What counts for the obsessional, on this score, is that his imaginary world – both that of his childhood and of his daily life – remains unaltered. Everything and everyone must stay where they are! The great risk is that the analyst, too, may find a place there and stay in it forever, as in the Museé Grévin.

Usually, the obsessional will present us with a caricature of the parental couple, which seems to be designed to create obsessionals: an omnipresent, protecting mother, who is distant and yet insists on over-feeding, even stuffing the child; an ogre of a father, but who toes the line when his other half is around, etc., etc.

What surprises me is that analysts tend to take these caricatures so seriously. When a hysteric tells us that her father tried to seduce her, we immediately think: fantasy, projection, screen memory, etc. But it is not only the hysteric who invents her history, who "hystorises"; the obsessional does it just as much.

So, I discern a curious credulity in analysts, one could even say, the return of a suspect type of geneticism under the cover of the real.

The relation of the obsessional to trauma is not amnesia, as it is for the hysteric. Amnesia leaves a hole in the narrative and consequently puts down a marker, opens up a pathway that can lead towards the knowledge of what counts.

The obsessional never forgets, but he makes things ordinary, he makes them smooth. We may ask if that does not impel analysts towards such a thing as an "objective" discourse. Basically, we may go as far as to believe that the obsessional is describing the real to us.

But this is not where we will find the real, certainly not in a description of the parents' roles. While there is a primary jouissance for the obsessional upon which he founds his nostalgia and his quest, it is in no way related to a historical event. It is because jouissance as such is traumatic, and it is impossible to aim at jouissance unless this aim is based upon an irreparable loss.

The neurotic does not have a choice: either he aims at jouissance and risks becoming obsessional, or he aims at desire and runs the risk of hysteria. Obviously, he could become perverse. But the neurotic – especially the obsessional – dreams of being perverse because he imagines that the pervert controls jouissance. This is not true. On the contrary, the jouissance of the pervert comes precisely at the price of submission to the jouissance of the Other. And I would add that if we want to be logical where the fantasy and its structure are concerned, we have to base it on the following premise: it is obsessional neurosis, the structure, that produces the history – and not the other way around. At least it is what produces the history as told to us by the analysand at the beginning of analysis. Obviously, the history that he re-finds at the end of his analysis, that which he interprets and reconstructs, is something else. In fact, it is still not the real; it is, I would say, quite simply the history of the subject, the history on the basis of which his desire can find its cause and its field of deployment.

So, the fundamental question would rather be: why is it that with the obsessional, unlike with the hysteric, we are tempted to take this imaginary narrative that he brings to us for the real? Why is there always this slippery slope, in any treatment of obsessional neurosis, which leads us to be duped by his imaginary? It seems to me that there is a fairly simple explanation for this, which is that what the obsessional tells us may seem to assume an apparent objectivity since he, the subject, absents himself from it. Well, I think it would be just as much an error to take his imaginary for the unique locus of his subjectivity, as it would be, *a contrario*, to neglect his puppet theatre all together. It would be just as debatable to take his ego and his objects for the very enunciation of his fantasy as it would be to think that there was no relation at all between them.

To put it another way, if the imaginary is prevalent for the obsessional, if it constitutes an obstacle to the subject's symbolic markers, this imaginary is, on the other hand, not without signification. This does not mean that it can be interpreted; and that is the difficulty I am going to explore now.

The obsessional offers us his imaginary world full of sound and fury, of hate and love, of suffering and disillusionment, so that we will get lost, like Tom Thumb in the forest. But at the same time, and because he is in analysis, because he found himself in the subjective disarray we have seen, and because he is under the transference, this world is the place where he can struggle under the gaze the Other. Through the way he lives, the obsessional keeps on showing his castration, in order to give the Other something to look at. You might say that the more he tries to draw us in and the more he seeks to hypnotise us, the more he himself becomes caught in the same trap: the more he becomes embroiled in acting-out. And he is constantly acting-out, because it is a way for him to make the Other exist and keep him as the cause of his jouissance.

This is why we cannot neglect his imaginary. It may be disconcerting, when he stops speaking to us, signalling to us that he has pushed us out of the place of the Other, from which place nonetheless we are still keeping an eye on him, if I may put it that way. This raises the question of the place of the analyst for us, in so far as it is from this place that a direction of the treatment is possible.

The obsessional goes to see an analyst in order to make him into a master, a master of jouissance. He hopes that his relation to jouissance will be pacified, distributing it differently, legalising his phallic jouissance so that under that cloak he can dedicate himself to his passionate ignorance of the Other's jouissance. He binds himself to his analyst, and binds the analyst to himself – ties him up – in a sort of treaty of non-aggression; and as is the case with any contract of this nature, it is supported by reciprocal complicity, often on the back of a third party. The third party here is the Other, this Other who is supposed to close his eyes and stay well away from jouissance.

Of course, just because the obsessional puts the analyst in this place, it doesn't mean he has to stay there. The question is, how can the analyst not play dead? Leclaire raised this question, and he concluded that it was perhaps the least bad way of conducting the treatment of an obsessional; part of his reasoning was that one should not stir up murky waters. This at least shows an element of prudence. What I have put forward regarding acting-out and the relation to anxiety, in the sense of how present these are for the obsessional, means that this position has some value. But the usual outcome of this is interminable analysis, each of the parties (analysand and analyst) waiting for the other to die first – this time for real.

Lacan did not always come to the same conclusion on this question of the place of the analyst. Up till the beginning of the 1960s, he put the analyst in the place of the Other: "It is only owing to the place of the Other that the analyst can receive the investiture of the transference that qualifies him to play his legitimate role in the subject's unconscious…" (Lacan, 1966, p. 379). But assigning the analyst to the place of the Other calls for a few observations.

First of all, this is consistent with Lacan's doctrine as it was constituted at the time, and the most important word in this quotation is "legitimate". The legitimacy of the position of the analyst comes to him on the basis of the notion that the law of desire is the foundation of the structure of the Other. But the analyst cannot abuse this place of the Other, because the Other himself is subject to the dialectic of desire. And what fundamentally justifies Lacan in saying this is the Name-of-the-Father, the paternal metaphor, which is the sole well-spring of phallic signification; during this period, Lacan spoke of the law of speech. Speech as a whole obeys the paternal metaphor and phallic signification. The function of the analyst also obeys this law, and we can say that the analyst operates, intervenes, acts, and interprets in the name of the father – under its banner.

It is the Name-of-the-Father, and the paternal metaphor which it commands, that legitimises the analyst and which orientates his act, because it is the compass he uses to find the way back to the path of desire. It seems to me that we can see here why and above all, how, it is that analysis can suit the obsessional. In so far as it is a father he is appealing to, he comes to analysis, in fact, so that his relation to desire can be brought to light. He is not at all delighted that this desire appears to him to be impossible. Clearly, he suffers because of this. The only thing is, he does not realise that his desire is impossible in order to protect him from the jouissance he wants to know nothing of, the jouissance of the Other. He expects the father to lay down the law regarding jouissance, in other words to forbid it, so that it will be possible for him to desire in peace, sheltered by the phallus. After all, this legitimation of desire is more or less consistent with what Lacan was saying about until the 1960s.

The only thing is, from the moment when the a is completely dissociated from the $-\varphi$, a becomes the cause of desire. The $-\varphi$ is not sufficient to maintain the connection between desire and the real of sex, unless, as he puts it (in "Subversion of the subject and the dialectic of desire"

(Lacan, 1966, pp. 671–702)), it manages to imaginarise the subject in the fantasy. It is not the object cause of desire that is sexuated (the *a* has no sex), it is the subject $; from then on, if the object cause of desire is desexualised, where will we find the real of sex, since there are two of them? What will be the effect on the subject of the absence of the sexual relation? The effect it has is this: it operates on jouissance, by dividing it, by dissociating phallic jouissance from the jouissance of the Other, from this Other who will now incarnate sexual otherness.

This of course has consequences. The major consequence is that the limits of the paternal metaphor are put in place, the limits of interpretation in the name of the father. This is why, progressively, Lacan will dislodge the analyst from the position of the Other, and will end up putting him in the position of the semblance, since that is where object *a* is located.

All this talk of the semblance has taken us a long way from the legitimacy of the signifier. In fact, the analyst does have to maintain an irreducible semblance. Obviously, there is a difference between occupying this place through the signifier itself, or through the object cause of desire. The signifier as such is the semblance proper (it is only ever the name of the thing, never the thing itself). And, in this respect, it is indeed in the discourse of the master that the imposture comes closest. Inserting the object *a* here is something else, all the more so since Lacan did not stop at designating it "cause of desire", and went on to call it *"plus de jouir"*, surplus jouissance. In other words, he made it equivalent to jouissance itself, the jouissance by which the Other, the Other of the Signifier, the big Other, is deserted.

So, what is the meaning of the displacement of the analyst as *A* [Other] to analyst as *a*? And in whose name does the analyst interpret, if he no longer does so in the name of the father? Answer: he interprets by relying on the object, in the name of the object. And we must be more precise: if we say he interprets in the name of the object cause of desire, it could refer again to phallic signification because in the case of neurosis desire can be well satisfied to be ruled by the phallus. The difference is not yet emphasised when the analyst is in the position of *A*. But it becomes more marked when the *a* designates jouissance, surplus jouissance. I will explain what I mean by focussing on this question of interpretation.

An interpretation is based on the model of the metaphor, which means that it consists in bringing a repressed element into signification.

This is what Lacan called "crossing the bar", and the effect is the emergence of signification. If you take the writing of the discourses, it seems that interpretation consists in making something move from the position of truth (something which, by dint of being in that position, has taken on the value of truth) to the position of agent:

$$\frac{\$}{a} \quad \leftarrow \quad S2 \qquad \frac{a}{S2} \rightarrow \$$$

$$\frac{\$}{a} \quad \xrightarrow{\quad} \quad \frac{a}{S2}$$

In other words, any analytic interpretation concerns jouissance: the impossible gap that separates the subject from his object. Because desire is phallic, it makes jouissance possible, but not all jouissance; and analytic interpretation consists in bringing this difference into play, this distinction between $-\varphi$ and a, between castration which regulates jouissance as possible, and the object a which reveals the impossibility of it. The place of the analyst can then be situated in this gap that appears in the antinomy between desire and jouissance, between a as cause of desire and a as surplus jouissance. Well, we have seen that the obsessional places the demand of the Other in this gap; and it is what gives him jouissance on condition that he gives up on his desire.

Conversely, he may recognise his desire on condition that he makes it impossible. More than the hysteric, he accentuates the incompatibility between desire and jouissance. It is one of the foundations – one of many – of these eternal choices, of these constant duplications we find in his existence. The obsessional always arrives bearing an either/or in his arms: either I give in to the desire of the Other or I don't. Thus, the analyst always has a central marker according to which he can situate himself: he has to use this demand of the Other as his guiding mark. His response is not to incarnate the Other; but nor should he do the opposite and protect the subject from it.

Clearly, it is much more soothing to aim at a pacification of this alienating alternative. To do this, to silence the demand of the Other, it suffices to add a dose of the law of desire, in other words, of the phallic order. It is quite amusing to tell oneself that protestations against this order are always made by hysterics; and yet the question is quite different for them, since they are the ones who impose this order, and it is much easier for the analyst to realise that there is no need to add any more for them. In short, what will pacify the obsessional is an analyst who makes himself the upholder of the phallic order, incarnating the imaginary father.

The obsessional's either/or can soon be dealt with: it becomes a neither/nor. This is a caricature, of course, but it shows how the treatment may become obsessionalised. But, conversely, incarnating the demand of the Other may not suffice to bring all the difficulties under control. In the same way one should not confuse the demand of the Other with straightforward ego reinforcement, the push-to-performance that Lacan observed in the *Écrits*, which would rather call for the analyst to show nothing but indifference. But that is not the real difficulty, the one which leads analysts to opt for peace and quiet. The real difficulty is that, if the demand of the Other creates a gap between desire and jouissance, it is because their conjunction causes anxiety in the obsessional. And in the end, it seems to me, this is the real risk in the analysis of the obsessional. Because once he becomes anxious, there is no stopping him. It is another form of reinforcement, a much more trying one: when he appears to be bent on pure dereliction, on wrecking everything.

It is difficult to choose between a peaceful analysis, in which the obsessional allows himself plenty of acting-out and in which it suffices for him that the Other frowns on his actions, and, on the other hand, an analysis in which surplus jouissance is right in his face, to the extent that it may drive him to pass to the act. And yet it seems to me that anxiety is a risk we must take if interpretation is to have its effect of signification.

So, Lacan's term "the direction of the treatment" should not, I believe, be understood in the sense that the analyst would be the one to direct the treatment, but rather that he would have a clear sense of its aims – that he would know where it was going. There is certainly no such thing as mastery of this direction; but he can try to be one step ahead of the analysand, gently showing him where to tread next; and this is because he, the analyst, has a compass. It is to the extent that the analyst knows what comes into the position of truth that he can hoist it in the place of the semblance. Mastery is the opposite of what Lacan calls the desire of the analyst. And the place of mastery is where the obsessional expects the analyst to be, in the transference, in the transference as love. And when Lacan refers to a "reverse hypnosis" in the sense that the transference puts the analyst in the position of the one being hypnotised, that seems to me particularly apposite where the obsessional is concerned.

Not because the analyst falls asleep – not just because of that, in any case – but because, faced with the obsessional patient, far more than where a hysteric is concerned, the analyst is necessarily led to wonder, "But what does he want of me? What is he expecting from me?"

It is too easy to reply: "He wants me to die," even if it is true, or, "He wants me to keep quiet". I believe rather that the obsessional expects the analyst to reject him, not in the sense of aggressivity or hate, but in the sense of being an object. He seems to say to the analyst: "I'll come until you get rid of me, so that after that you can desire me; so that after all you will desire because of me." To my mind, this radical inversion explains what we sometimes notice in terms of the obsessional's passivity, docility, even of passive homosexuality. Beyond the demand of the Other, the obsessional accedes to the desire of the Other when he can overcome his anxiety, but he can only accede to it from one place: the place from which he can cause desire. This, I would say, is a hazard that emerges later on in the treatment. Transference love is a call to desire, but only on condition that he can make himself the reject, the unclaimed article, of this desire.

So, this is the rather perilous way in which an obsessional can become an analyst. It may even be the prospect of this position of being a piece of rubbish that leads him to become an analyst. It is not clear that it is necessarily a good idea to encourage him. However, I think it is important to point out that this disposition of the obsessional is often masked by the famous identification with the analyst. It is not an identification with the analyst per se, but rather with the function he attributes to the latter: that of being the cause of desire, and with the advantage he supposes that the analyst gains from that: obtaining jouissance from it.

He will soon be disappointed, if he takes the step over to the analyst's chair; and that is why we often hear the complaint coming from obsessionals who have made that move precipitately, when they realise with astonishment just how little jouissance they get out of it, and how little assurance they find there with regard to their own desire. It's the wrong way for them to go, we may say, because their fantasy is still intact. And we have to acknowledge that it is not always possible to dislodge the obsessional from that position which we may call "pre-ending", from that last entrenchment before leaving analysis. The position in which he understands that the only thing one can do to accede to the desire of the Other is to make oneself its object.

I am not sure if this hazard can be avoided in every case. This is an awkward question because this final entrenchment, the ultimate ruse of analysis, is strictly linked to the analysis itself – it is an effect of it. It is even more awkward when we realise that this obstacle at the same time constitutes a possible means of access to the analyst's chair. Let me give you an illustration: the obsessional enters into the analytic discourse as object *a*, but he denies that it is a semblance; since obviously it is because this place belongs to the semblance that the analyst cannot extract any jouissance from occupying it. The obsessional refutes the existence of the semblance precisely in order to preserve his jouissance. The object *a* he uses as a support remains that of his fantasy and not that of the analysand.

Furthermore, we need to recognise that the obsessional is not necessarily any less adept than anyone else at occupying this place, but we should not be surprised to find that he suffers from it more than others; this suffering appears to me to be an avatar of the jouissance he gains from it. And it is thanks to this that he is not an imposter; on the contrary, he never stops worrying about making sure that he is not, and if I may say so, making sure that he pays with his person, that somehow or other he rewards the analysand who gives him the opportunity for this masochistic jouissance.

On this score, the end of analysis for an obsessional is particularly delicate. When the analyst is concerned to dislodge him from that place, it becomes a never-ending ending. There is no symptom anymore; desire is apparently in place and he knows where it is; and yet things are still not right. It is a false separation. And it is on how we understand the term "separation" that the question rests. It would be an error to rush into thinking of this separation as equivalent to the separation of analyst and analysand. Here, "separation" means separating oneself from the object *a*. But it is not because the surplus jouissance, the object of the fantasy, is a piece of rubbish, a reject, that the "fall of the fantasy" is equivalent to detaching oneself from the object. In the "Proposition of October 1967" (Lacan, 1995), Lacan said more or less the contrary: It is not the object that falls, but the subject. And it is precisely because the fantasy falls that the subject has to decide whether he wants to hold on to this object as a surplus jouissance or not.

On these grounds, subjective destitution does not mean throwing one's object *a* into the rubbish bin; rather, it means holding on to it, even if one has noticed that it was only a piece of rubbish. On that basis, separation can be conceived of as separation not from the signifier, but rather from the signifying chain in so far as it secures the subject to a conventional signification considered to be a norm. For the obsessional, it is even more essential that this securing is obviously, above all, guaranteed by the Name-of-the-Father; and in the end it is this that he does not want to let go of. For the obsessional, holding on to the Name-of-the-Father translates into his attachment to his "particular signifiers".

Note

1. This paper was first published in 2002 in *Revue Nationale des Collèges cliniques du Champ lacanien*: 135–156, with a preface by Danièle Silvestre who also gave permission for the paper to be translated into English and published in this book. [Ed.]

References

Freud, S. (1912–1913). *Totem and Taboo. S. E. ,13*: vii–162. London: Hogarth, 1953.

Freud, S. (1913i). The disposition to obsessional neurosis. *S. E., 12*: 311–326. London: Hogarth, 1958.

Lacan, J. (1966). *Écrits*. B. Fink (Trans.). New York: Norton, 2002.

Lacan, J. (1995). Proposition of the 9th October 1967 on the psychoanalyst of the school. R. Grigg (Trans.). *Analysis, 6*: 1–13.

CHAPTER EIGHT

There is a stain on the horizon
A loop or two into obsessional neurosis

VINCENT DACHY

Introductory portrait: the scope of a caricature –
whoops! – of a character

It may very well be that, within discourses of certain persuasions, recent classifications have not retained "obsessional neurosis" as a clinical entity. Amongst other reasons, could this disregard signal our attunement with this common neurosis, or even "pathological" entity? If it is not the place here to (re)consider what "pathology" may be, we shall nevertheless address the framework of this particular defensive arrangement characterised by an array of facets, the core articulation of which may escape those who like to believe in the positivity of "behaviours" or "cognitive awareness", and their supposedly direct relation to truth.

Indeed, how can we conjugate the following verbs understood as "actions", "methods", "procedures" of speaking-beings for whom "obsession" is the symptomatic fulcrum of their defensive arrangement? To cancel, delete, efface, erase; to wait, postpone, defer; to disaffect, drain, avoid, void; to doubt, ruminate, retain; to think, calculate, make sure, verify; to mortify, hate, destroy? This is an art of living, a *modus vivendi* that amounts to a brutal – even if subdued – constriction of living itself.

Rather than expanding on an extensive and involved phenomenology, we will try to differentiate several levels through which obsessional neurosis becomes organised.

First loop: carousel of transformations

From character to symptom: there is trouble in the routine

The *anal* attribute and the *anal character* have now entered common language and they have become practically synonymous with the "obsessional character", despite the disappearance of *obsessional neurosis*[1] from the psycho-psychiatric dominant discourses of our society. Although this *anal character* has some relevance, it truncates and demeans the scope of obsessional neurosis. When this disposition can be *anal,* namely meticulous, ordered, etc., it can just as well be rather flamboyant, boastful, and provocative, or urbanely hypocritical; just as discreet as ambitious or pretentious; just as placid as irritable and cantankerous, miserly or generous, self-controlled or bursting with rage, hesitant and cautious or gambling with money if not with his (or your) life, not expressing his emotions or rambling on about them (with, perhaps, an accentuation of reproaches to himself or, more often, to others). In brief, there are both many characteristic traits and their opposites. As specific symptoms can easily be integrated in the general character (considered as an amalgamation of ego and modes of satisfaction) we hypothesise, taking on board the crucial role of reaction-formations,[2] that the primary motives of the formation of character are those linked to symptoms. One specific obsession (being everywhere on time, exactly on the dot, to take a banal example) may indeed become a personality trait, which the subject and his entourage learn to live with more or less at ease, making it a virtue or ruining every single holiday departure. Symptoms themselves have a broad scope: procedures or rituals of thoughts and of actions; endless doubtful inquiries to "make sure", distrustful verifications; compulsions to do things which the subject disapproves of; more or less extreme difficulty to make decisions – and keep to them; hateful and violent thoughts (directed to loved ones on occasion), resultant feelings of guilt; severe anxiety about hurting people or of saying, doing scandalous, offensive, inappropriate things; dearth of emotions; paralysing feelings about the imminence of a catastrophe (which they may or may not fend off by countering actions which themselves may bring undesirable consequences and which, therefore, will have to be managed by further painstaking measures, etc.) The subject often experiences doubts (uncertainty >< decision)[3] about himself, others and potentially anything, feels guilty (fault >< responsibility), which, quite frequently, does not sufficiently curb the anxiety (enjoyment (jouissance)> <desire) whose manifestations surface in various guises (hesitations, hypochondria, sudden bursts of angst, "lack of confidence", etc.) The subject, often in concealed ways, will spend considerable time controlling himself, his actions, impulses, feelings, thoughts, etc., and tell himself off: "you must ...", "you ought to ...", "you only have to ...", "you should ...", "you shall ...". "Compulsion" is transformed into "compulsory."

The obsessional speaking-being? An incarnation of the principle of (self)conscience.

From symptom to fantasy: from disruption to supposition

The symptoms, stretched between uninvited spillages and measures to stay irreproachably in control, can give access to the territory of fantasy. These fantasies, whatever their variations and the degrees of their ascendancy, fluctuate between the subjugation to an experience of enjoyment and the enjoyment of an experience of subjugation.

From fantasy to drives: under their sway

The variations of fantasies could be brought to an overall formulation which gives a grammatical and logical frame, a casing to a conglomeration of drives issued from encountering a void.

What about that (initial) encounter? E-vent in the body

The encounter with sexuality is cutting, traumatic for everyone: it happens as an ineffaceable discontinuity. This encounter – a body-event – is experienced as imposed. For the obsessional subject, the encounter is welcomed as the experience is enjoyed (in contrast with hysteria), and, yet, the subject experiences it as "too much", a "too much of pleasure", as Freud said.[4] Too much, not necessarily because of some possible "abuse", but because the subject is not "in charge" of its initial occurrence, and because it does not solve the problem of satisfaction altogether. The local enjoyment (jouissance) does not lead to any global solution. Enjoyment remains a puzzle within the problematic field of satisfaction. The local, partial sexual enjoyment does not settle the relation to sexuality or the sexual relation. The enjoyment remains a local experience, and therefore does not solve the discontinuity between enjoyment (partial, incomplete) and desire (sustained by a compensating fantasy of completion): a disjunction called castration.

From drive to fantasy: sheathing sheaves

The drives that are integrated by the fantasy derive from the void encountered through the subjugation to a genital-phallic enjoyment. As a matter of fact, that encounter, albeit enjoyable, presents the subject with the silence of the Other. The Other does not swear by or to, transmit, or write down the sexual relation. To deal with that void, the fantasy will integrate and conglomerate the drives under a supposition, axiomatise the drives which have already given some density to the void around which they revolve. To overcome the insisting disjunction, to make it cohere, to bridge the sexual relation encountered as a solution of continuity, a palliation is found, in the case of obsessional neurosis, either in an anal retreat or in a scopic venture.[5] The former tries to (re-) establish continuity by debasing desire into demand, to which the anal object gave form and intensity (the Other demands, enjoins, orders – irrespective of whether the subject complies or rebels), while the latter attempts to cover the subjective split with the gaze which gives consistency to the power of thinking.[6]

The fantasy forms a passage from the experience of a local puzzling enjoyment to an overall belief about enjoyment, by forming a personal myth, a belief based on the drives; the fantasy attempts to compensate for the disjunction.

From fantasy to symptom: something fails (again), therefore protocol, procedure, regulation ... rituals

But the fantasy does not resolve the disjunction, it does not compensate for it without inconsistencies. These "discrepancies" of the fantasy trying to write the sexual relation, failing to regulate consistently the disjunction which, meanwhile, the persisting, pressing drives carry on testing (and testifying to), produce compromise(s) between general belief and local insistence, to which the symptoms in their veracious varieties [*varité*] will bear witness. These symptoms often have a magico-religious or a bureaucratic dimension (the latter especially when elements of logic get mingled with it), trying to reduce if not extinguish a failure through rituals and procedures.

From symptom to globalisation

These symptoms which are often conflated in the "character", in the *modus operandi* of an individual, will also fit like a glove discourses that privilege exploitation, banknotes and return, on the one hand, and exploits, note and renown on the other.

Nota bene: the passage from symptom to drive has not been mentioned in the carousel above. From the point of the symptom we can either go to fantasy or to drives. Symptoms have always a component of drive associated with them, which is clearly present in the fact that despite symptoms being disruptive, one does not know how to live without them. Symptoms disclose the link between local and global, and the disparity between them.

Second loop: the problem, the defensive arrangement

The problem: too much of a good thing is nevertheless too much

If we consider castration as a disjunction between enjoyment and desire in as far as the speaking being encounters not only the problem of satisfaction in relation to the Other and the body but, also, in the encounter with sexual difference and the satisfaction(s) from (around, fanning from, echoing) the genital zone, then the speaking body encounters an enjoyment – passively (welcoming it or not subsequently), and the "silence" of the Other (whatever the Other may say at this juncture, a vent remains that does not bridge the local enjoyment with the global problem of satisfaction).[7]

If, in psychoanalysis, many things have been said about dissatisfaction, lack, etc., the obsessional subject reminds us that for all speaking beings it is always an excess (as '*too* much' or '*too* much of not enough') that impels some defensive arrangement.

The defence: the stain that washes whiter

The imposition of life, language, sexual difference, and the problem of satisfaction that ensues (*viz* the problems of/with enjoyment), is something to which the obsessional subject reacts in his own way. This imposition of enjoyment to which the obsessional subject is subjugated is what will come back to him in the form of constraint, of compulsion. Inversely, the disjunction between enjoyment and desire (echoing the vent between *das Ding* of enjoyment and *die Sache* of desire[8]) is invested for itself as deferral of the encounter between desire and enjoyment (avoidance of castration), and that postponement is placed under the "auspices of impossibility". In the context of desiring – of non-realised satisfaction invested for itself in and by language (symbolised as want, lack) – the obsessional struggles with the subjugating imposition of enjoyment. He uses desire indexed with impossibility in order not to be arrested by the enjoyment to which he has assented – believing that, in doing so, he would become its master. Faced with castration, and grounded in the enjoyment in the body, the obsessional takes the position of being responsible for it, which is a way to manage his anxiety *vis-à-vis* castration. The obsessional shows how a degree of "sadism" is a treatment of the primary imposition (akin to "primary masochism").[9]

The operation of deleting fits in here. Here is a sketch. Somewhere, sometime, a spillage inadvertently happens to someone, and a st(r)ain ensues. Of course, this stain is indelible. How can it be got rid of? Most importantly, how is it possible to conceal (con-seal) the fact that the stain happened "unconsciously", disruptively as a blunder, a slip-up, as a smirch in the "first place"? This is where the obsessional arrangement goes beyond the obvious and superficial sponge, scrub or disinfection (see anal character → cleanliness, etc.) The truly sagacious method is to make another stain over the first one, voluntarily this time, and, thereby, claiming responsibility, deleting the very division produced by the "first" stain.[10]

If death occupies a special place in the ideations of the obsessional and paves the way to his dramatisation (albeit subdued), it is, first and foremost, as a version of the mort-ification of desiring. Death is a figure for neutralisation: *nothingification*. Death: *d*eath considered as *the* horizon,[11] inaccessible, always for tomorrow (until *the* last day), appealing or appalling but out of reach, crucial but never putting your back against the wall (until *the* last moment). The impossibility of reaching the horizon is useful to delay the hour of the realisation of desire, which would confront him with the actual impossibility: the resolution of the disjunction intrinsic to satisfaction, from which enjoyment ensues, and "repeated" in the disjunction between enjoyment and desire. The obsessional arrangement puts the non-possibility into play in lieu of the recusal of the possibility of junction, leaving him conjugating (ad, con, in, inter, sub-) junctions.[12] But, coincidently, the disjunction is always potentially imminent (and anxiety easily prompted), contingently possible. The encounter with the accidental, the non-eliminable possibility of a contingent disruption, the non-calculable happening, *the* catastrophe remains always a threat. Contingency, in experience, embodies the impossibility (as recusal) of the exhaustion of possibilities, in thinking. No wonder that death is so ordinarily present to the obsessional's mind as it is both a figure of castration (figure of impossibility-certainty in relation to which the subject can only be impotent[13]), and of ultimate mastery of enjoyment (figure of a local enjoyment attaining its global exhaustion, "the moment that lasts forever"). It is possible to use an absolute notion (death) to conceal a relative problem (the disjunction), possible to sustain an absolute while staying clear from any of its relative incarnations.[14]

Delete (space) - delay (time).

Once again (just to make sure): to avoid a void in the vent of an event

The double operation expounded above elucidates why obsessional neurosis is a defence against enjoyment both as excess and as failure. It is important to grasp this double operation so as not to miss the dignity of the whole defensive arrangement altogether.

The obsessional operation repeats the crucial initial moment:

1. there is imposition.
2. the subject takes it upon himself. That is his *proton-pseudos*.[15]

What is, thereby, effaced is the primary 'involuntary will', the obliteration of the origin. The subject appears in time 2, as effect of time 1, but tries to get back on its feet as superintendent of time 1, an operation akin to the so often observed attempt to reduce to a statement what appears first as an enunciation. As Lacan said, the obsessional spends considerable time trying to find the sign in, behind, underneath the signifier

(1962–1963, p. 62); he struggles to find what represents something for someone behind what divides the "someone"; division which, at the level of signifiers, manifests the disjunction, Δ, between enjoyment as "it should be", Ej, and enjoyment as "it is experienced", Φ. Ej Δ Φ.[16] The obsessional would like to be a behaviourist, and make the sign the witness of a straightforward causality, simple, straightforward, observable, and indisputable between language and satisfaction, without detours through enjoyment. Above all, the obsessional would like to go back to the origin from which he could start afresh, back to square one, from a position of non-subjugation, a position of control and will – position of the decider, of the (self-)"determinator", despite the heavy price he may pay for it.[17] The obsessional attempts to make the failure fail. If it is impossible not to fail, the obsessional tries to make the impossible not fail ... To make the impossible a possibility, and consider some possibilities as impossible ... [18]

The anxiety of the obsessional is linked to this impossible "authorship" of enjoyment. As speaking bodies, we do not decide our origin, neither where nor from whom we happen to be born. How can we be the master of what has produced us? Taking responsibility is not enough: the obsessional wants to be the instigator, even at the price of being the culprit, which perhaps is not pleasant, although it is not impossible to derive some pride from it, but anything is better than being the effect of the will of the Other. The imposition of the verb is not impersonal but is linked to the will of the Other, its power, its default ultimately. Hence the passion of the obsessional to kill off any occurrence of enjoyment of the Other. The enjoyment of the Other is most unacceptable to the obsessional subject because it is in the Other that the obsessional subject hopes to solve the disjunction which never ceases to interpellate him. Hatred easily rises for the agency of the Other which is relied upon, because there is always something that squirms, dies of something, throbs, again and always. The Other is desired as dead but the tomb is never totally empty, clean and proper. Should we therefore be surprised to see that the problem of creation(ism) formulated in terms of *creator* versus *creature*, *increated* versus *created* may bother the obsessional, especially in his perspicacity as theologican? The obsessional will go to great lengths to bring the Other's enjoyment into the rails of consistent logic, of proper conduct, of immaculate conception. Let him be called Calvin, Cromwell, Frege or Baden Powell, there are many ways to remind a pope, an American president, a speculator, a child, or any ordinary citizen of his deportment! As history shows, such passionate cutting to size may come with its own excesses, its own defensive oppressions ...

Tinkering thinking, refuge of normalised pusillanimity

The obsessional thinks, and shows us how thinking, aside from its marvellous productions to which civilisation bears witness, has its roots firmly planted in the problem of satisfaction.[19] He strings enjoyment through signifiers which he triturates, with which he fiddles, trying to reduce enjoyment to the stringing. Relentlessly, he attempts to get enjoyment assimilated into signifying webs. The obsessional can be a masterful nit-picker, quick to reply when questioned, agile at defending, often witty, swift to escape corners, astute at clouding issues. His wielding of the various uses of negation can amount to virtuosity. But all is not well with this robust eschewal that runs into the drive which is unfazed by negation. And yet, thinking, despite its ultimate lack of consistence, is a powerful derivative and a formidable spillway of sublimation. Thinking is also a great help to sustain inhibition while pursuing a life of intimate kinks and private convolutions. Although the obsessional is not always paralysed into inaction, when the hour of his desire comes, he may choose the route of the exploit, yet more often will prefer some adjournment. The obsessional's disposition aims at the total explicitation of the implicit but only finds inconsistency which fuels his procrastination, and incompleteness beyond. His scientistic or religious convictions (as opposite forces to doubt) that strive at reducing the implicit to some explicitation – all clear! – can become destructive, deadening. When clarifications meet their limitations, they can easily lead to clearance, and to cleansing ... The obsessional is not known for his inclination to cross the Rubicon but he can have his moment of intrepidity. Such is his dislike of inconsistency, and his horror of incompleteness.

Camouflage of the obsessional in the prevalent social ideal

Finding a social authorisation for his arrangement in a socially constituted and accepted discourse is what the obsessional arrangement has found in various forms of puritanism.[20] And through the gradual blunting of puritanism the obsessional arrangement can easily get in tune with a capitalism, which sees in "success" the approval of a demiurge. Capitalism, we propound, is not simply a particular way of benefiting

from exploitation (which some of its supporters use to justify its natu-
ralness) but a more complicated operation: the production/creation of
surplus, of the gain that is extracted from the exploitation of exploitation (the operation of usury is a seminal example, or the exploitation
of labour time – making a commodity out of a reification, without even
mentioning the exploitation of the possession of means of production).
Would this operation of doubling be akin to the operation described
above whereby the obsessional extracts an enjoyment from obliterating
the primary enjoyment to which he consented? Who is relentlessly on
the lookout for surplus-gain, growth, and also finds some meaningful
techno-scientific or religious meaningful, if not redemptive, justification for it? Who has not noticed the affinity between capitalism and
anal investment? Refuse, garbage, shittiness, not in themselves but in
their asymptotic accrual. Who has not noticed the affinity between capitalism and scopic investment? Surveillance, comparison, competition,
success, not in themselves but in their forced validation. Both anal and
scopic investments, together with a particular movement between having and being – having (money, for instance) leading to being (being
someone, at least a recognised image),[21] tightly scaffold the disjunction
which the obsessional does not want to encounter. Having been a frog
flushed with enjoyment, he wants to become a gleaming ox. Who is
the champion of capitalism? But there is an intrinsic failure when it
comes to the establishment of a stable, fixedly regulated, written passage between potency and enjoyment. Who does not know the danger
of inflation?

There is a too-much, a bonus that is too much but I can't resist it even
if ... Too much of "goods" proves to be too much. Perhaps are we all too
used to the most ordinary neurosis?

Let us remain attentive that the obsessional would not endorse a master, a master whom he may very well deem stupid, as an authorisation,
a relieving caution for his own mental debasement (good → goods) and
timorousness (voidance → avoidance).

Usual, all too usual?

Notes

1. See Freud, 1908b, Character and anal erotism.
2. Reaction-formation: counter-cathexis, counter-investment. See, for
   instance, Freud, 1926d, *Inhibitions, Symptoms and Anxiety*.

3. The symbol > < means: "in tension with", "in conflict with"; e.g., doubt as a result of tension between uncertainty and decision.

4. See Freud, 1887–1904, Letter 38; Letter 46. Freud, 1896a, Heredity and the aetiology of the neuroses. Freud, 1896b, Further remarks on the neuro-psychoses of defence. Freud, 1913i, The disposition to obsessional neurosis. Lacan, 1959–1960, *Seminar VII*, p. 54.

5. Lacan, for reasons linked to the illusion of a "natural", spontaneous, progressive, and staged maturation, did not promote the Freudian concept of regression (or an idea of progression for that matter). We put forward the ideas of "retreat" and "venture", which indicate a different dynamic around the void. Anal retreat: demand substituted for desire. Scopic venture: power swathing (im)potency.

6. Looking overlooks the gaze inasmuch as the gaze splits looking itself. Looking gives consistency to the Other's knowledge: the Other sees (everything) ≡ the Other knows (everything). Next, seeing becomes equivalent to thinking oneself thinking. Picture this thinking game: "I see that you see that I see that you see that ...", which gives an illusory coalescence between thinking and seeing, and the accompanying enjoyment of mastering power. Gaping at the split in the Other (in voyeuristic posture for instance), or "making oneself be" through the Other's gaze (making oneself seen), give an illusion of power over the subjective split.

   Let's not forget the voice present in the imperative which resonates in the demand. The oral drive seems the least apparent variation of the drive in this arrangement, unless, perhaps, it surfaces through an anxiety of "being eaten", taken over. Both the invocatory and oral drives come into play in rather discomforting manners that evoke the void, in contrast to the anal and scopic ways which try to conceal it.

7. That is why children, when explained the "facts of life", often find the "speech" rather strange if not ridiculous, or just simply unbelievable. Despite what the "adults" who may have ended up believing "the speech", may think, it never takes long to reach the incompleteness of sexual theories.

8. The object of desire, the object targeted by desire, which Lacan will re-situate as object-cause of desire, which indicates more clearly its "roots" in the *Ding* of enjoyment. *Das Ding*, the object-in-itself, noumenon; *die Sache*, the thing, matter, object, phenomenon.

9. As Lacan suggested (see Lacan, 1970–1971, *Le Séminaire*, Livre XVIII, séance du 9 & 16/06/71, pp. 161 and 177, not translated), the myth of

the Primal Horde referred to by Freud in *Totem and Taboo* (1912–1913) is an obsessional fantasy. The myth revolves around the enjoyment of the Other - making the father an exception to the universal lack. The "primal father" who possesses all-women is not touched by the disjunction. And the sons (what about the daughters?) kill him only to institute his homage. The myth strives for a symbolisation of the real void at the place of *the satisfaction that should have been*.

10. See Freud, 1909d, Notes upon a case of obsessional neurosis, pp. 190f, in which the so-called Rat Man removes a rock from the path that the stagecoach of his lady's carriage would follow, and then, realising the absurdity of his gesture, backtracks and puts it right back in its initial spot.

11. The horizon from which one can organise a belief. See G. Châtelet, *Les Enjeux du Mobile,* Seuil, Paris, 1993, pp. 83–96, (translated as *Science and Philosophy*, Springer, 1999).

12. We find traces of such alteration in respectable operations such as "reification", "hypostasis", "suture", even the conjuring of Frege to found arithmetic. Various very deft sleights of hands with erasure, impossibility and nothingness.

13. This is why, when it comes to this juggling with death, an analyst may have to distinguish a smoke screen from the burning flesh.

14. Here, one can perhaps glimpse the pathway leading to religions (the revealed ones, by preference).

15. In Aristotle, the link between false premises and false conclusions. See the *proton-pseudos* linked to hysteria by Freud, 1895 [1950a], in Project for a scientific psychology.

16. If a sign implies the representation (and possible absence) of the thing of which it is the sign, the signifier represents the absence of representation of the subject. The signifier bears witness to the division of the use of a sign between enunciation and statement, to the fact that a speaking body is concerned there but nowhere represented in itself.

    The order of signs may allure but the only difficulty with it is the disappearance ("nothingification", neutralisation, suture, etc.) of the subject, which could be bliss if it was not atrocious. (See Kafka's troublesome novels, or bureaucracy, scientism, cults, and marketing logics, for instance.)

17. What would Lady Macbeth say?

See the extraordinary *The Private Memoirs and Confessions of a Justified Sinner, Written by Himself: With a Detail of Curious Traditionary Facts and Other Evidence by the Editor* by J. Hogg, 1824.

18. If one thinks here of some philosophers of the twentieth century - amongst the best ones that is – it may not just be a coincidence.

19. If a *conversion* in the body operates in hysteria, the *conversion* in obsessional neurosis happens in thinking. About this contrast, see A. Chekhov, 1896, "The house with the mezzanine".

20. See Dachy, 2005.

21. [a → i(a)] $^{\varphi/\varphi}$, passage of the object *a* to the image of the other in a space bounded by the power of the phallic relation.

References

Châtelet, G. (1993). *Science and Philosophy*, Springer: New York, 1999.

Chekov, A. (1896). The house with the mezzanine. In: A. Chekov, *The Lady with the Little Dog and Other Short Stories, 1896–1904*. R. Wilks (Trans.). London: Penguin, 2002, pp. 3–22.

Dachy, V. (2005). Obsessional neurosis, puritanism, "funism" and psychoanalysis. *Journal of the Centre for Freudian Analysis and Research, 16:* 28–42.

Freud, S. (1887–1904). *The Complete Letters of Sigmund Freud to Wilhelm Fliess 1887–1904.* Cambridge, Mass.: Belknap, 1985.

Freud, S. (1895 [1950a]). Project for a scientific psychology. *S. E., 1:* 281–392. London: Hogarth, 1966.

Freud, S. (1896a). Heredity and the aetiology of the neuroses. *S. E., 3:* 140–156. London: Hogarth, 1962.

Freud, S. (1896b). Further remarks on the neuro-psychoses of defence. *S. E., 3:* 157–185. London: Hogarth, 1959.

Freud, S. (1908b). Character and anal erotism. *S. E., 9:* 167–175. London: Hogarth, 1959.

Freud, S. (1909d). Notes upon a case of obsessional neurosis, *S. E., 10:* 151–249. London: Hogarth, 1955.

Freud, S. (1912–1913). *Totem and Taboo. S. E., 13:* vii–162. London: Hogarth, 1953.

Freud, S. (1913i). The disposition to obsessional neurosis. *S. E.,12:* 311–326. London: Hogarth, 1958.

Freud, S. (1926b). *Inhibitions, Symptoms and Anxiety. S. E., 20:* 75–175. London: Hogarth, 1959.

Hogg, J. (1824). *The Private Memoirs and Confessions of a Justified Sinner, Written by Himself: With a Detail of Curious Traditionary Facts and Other*

Evidence by the Editor. J. Carey (Ed.). Cambridge: Cambridge University Press, 1970.

Lacan, J. (1959–1960). *The Seminar of Jacques Lacan, Book VII, The Ethics of Psychoanalysis.* J.-A. Miller (Ed.), D. Porter (Trans.). New York: Norton, 1992.

Lacan, J. (1962–1963). *The Seminar of Jacques Lacan, Book X, Anxiety.* J.-A. Miller (Ed.), A. Price (Trans.). Cambridge: Polity, 2014.

Lacan, J. (1970–1971). *Le Séminaire, Livre XVIII, D'Un discours qui ne serait pas du semblant.* J.-A. Miller (Ed.). Paris: Seuil, 2006.